"The author writes brilliantly about her uncle's life throughout the Nazi regime. She successfully engages the reader in the emotions and drama of this horrific period. It is a unique and remarkable story of a man's struggle for what he believed. Ultimately, he survived to live as a free man in America. This is a must-read page-turner."

Larry Klass, Retired Veteran, U.S. Army

"I am grateful Ms Shimon has shared her uncle's story, not only of physical survival but also of overcoming unbelievable adversities to build a new life. It is a powerful and compelling story that should be promoted in schools and read by all."

Faye Kilstein, Child of Auschwitz survivor, First Generation American

First
One In,
Last
One Out

MARILYN SHIMON

mB

MIRROR BOOKS

Published in Great Britain by Mirror Books in 2020

First published in the United States of America in 2017
by CreateSpace Independent Publishing Platform,
North Charleston, South Carolina

Mirror Books is part of Reach plc
10 Lower Thames Street
London EC3R 6EN

www.mirrorbooks.co.uk

Print ISBN 978-1-913406-33-2
eBook ISBN: 978-1-913406-32-5

Typeset by Danny Lyle

Printed and bound in Great Britain by
CPI Group (UK) Ltd, Croydon, CR0 4YY

A CIP catalogue record for this book is available from the British Library.

Every effort has been made to fulfil requirements with regard to
reproducing copyright material. The author and publisher will be
glad to rectify any omissions at the earliest opportunity.

1 3 5 7 9 10 8 6 4 2

Cover images: Alamy / Depositphotos

This book is dedicated to the memory of my Great-Uncle Murray (also known as Moishe, Moniek, Mondig, and Morris), a hero who was born on July 11, 1911, in Warsaw, Poland, and who died in 1996 in Los Angeles, California. His profound determination to survive during the brutal years of the Third Reich and his relentless drive to outsmart the Nazis provide valuable lessons in perseverance and courage to follow one's dreams.

I hope that my uncle's remarkable story will be passed on to future generations so that our children will realize the depth of cruelty humans are capable of, as well as the strength one can muster to overcome hardships, so mankind never suffers another Holocaust.

This book is also dedicated to the memory of my loving father, Martin Hirsch, a proud Jew who diligently served in the U.S. Army during World War II. My father's unwavering love, wisdom, and encouragement gave me the incentive to delve into this dark, ugly period of our history and to share my

Uncle Murray's story. I will always be grateful to my father for empowering me with this strength.

Additionally, I want to dedicate this book to my dear son, Roy, and to thank him for all the joy and sunshine he continues to bring into my life. I love you, Roy.

Lastly, I want to dedicate my book to all the victims of the Holocaust.

Acknowledgements

My mother and consultant, Shula Hirsch, deserves the credit for the inception of this book in the early 1960s. I feel honored that I could transform her vision into reality. Without her countless hours of suggestions and encouragement, I would not have been able to write my uncle's story.

I also wish to extend my heartfelt gratitude to my brother, Sheldon, for his assistance in editing and contributing valuable suggestions to the making of this book.

"It happened, therefore it can happen again: this is the core of what we have to say. It can happen, and it can happen everywhere."

Primo Levi, Italian Holocaust survivor, author

"To remain silent and indifferent is the greatest sin of all."

Elie Wiesel, Romanian Holocaust survivor, political activist, author

"For evil to flourish, it only requires good men to do nothing."

Simon Wiesenthal, Austrian Holocaust survivor, Nazi hunter, author

"The sad and horrible conclusion is that no one cared that the Jews were being murdered. This is the Jewish lesson of the Holocaust and this is the lesson which Auschwitz taught us."

Ariel Sharon, 11th prime minister of Israel

"First they came for the Socialists,
and I did not speak out—
Because I was not a Socialist.
Then they came for the Trade Unionists,
and I did not speak out—
Because I was not a Trade Unionist.
Then they came for the Jews,
and I did not speak out—
Because I was not a Jew.
Then they came for me—
and there was no one left
to speak for me."

Martin Niemöller, German anti-Nazi theologian, Lutheran pastor

"Those who cannot remember the past are condemned to repeat it."
George Santayana, philosopher, author

Contents

Preface

When one hears the word *Holocaust*, the first image that frequently comes to mind is Auschwitz concentration camp and the heinous murders that took place there between 1942 and 1945. While more than one million innocent Jews were brutally murdered at Auschwitz, the magnitude and scope of the Holocaust extend far beyond the gates of this massive killing facility. We must not close our eyes to any element of the Holocaust and assume that because it happened over 70 years ago, it cannot happen again.

Furthermore, an all-encompassing analysis of the Holocaust must include a study of each targeted individual from every religion and nationality affected by the Nazis' inhumane actions. It was discovered—far more than once thought—that over 45,000 camps and ghettos, including six death camps, were established throughout Eastern Europe. It is inconceivable how one individual, Adolf Hitler, could orchestrate and mastermind the systematic attempt to annihilate an entire group of people, successfully killing over six million Jews alone. There are no other images in mankind's violent history that stir greater repugnance than the image of Adolf Hitler.

Germany was a highly advanced country with educated, professional citizens prior to World War II. In fact, many of the German Nazis held graduate degrees. It is a catastrophe that Nazis didn't use all their advanced learning in a productive manner instead of using it to mastermind a mass murder. How did Germany, one of the most cultural and advanced nations in the world, transform into a country of murderers?

Although numerous memoirs have been published on the Holocaust, it is crucial that we continue to focus on each individual account and not overlook anyone's personal story. While each survivor's story may vary slightly, depending on where and when he or she was a prisoner, each offers another piece of the complex puzzle and helps provide a comprehensive account of the Holocaust—the murder of six million Jews. The atrocities and horrors must constantly be revisited for all succeeding generations to follow, especially since the first generation of survivors is now disappearing.

It is understandable that after 70 years of being inundated with heart-wrenching memories and emotional testimonies about the Holocaust, one might experience *Holocaust fatigue* and not want to pursue the subject further. We, as a highly sophisticated society, cannot allow this to happen.

Enough is never enough when it comes to remembering the worst atrocity in the history of mankind. There must never be closure on the Holocaust. It is our responsibility to continue the legacy and preserve as many testimonies as possible. If we bury the Holocaust, we will enable our enemies to commit further genocides, following in the footsteps of Adolf Hitler and the Nazi party.

My mother and father attended the trial of Adolf Eichmann in Jerusalem, Israel, in 1961. Eichmann, a major figure in the Holocaust, testified at his trial for crimes against humanity in Israel by stating:

"To be frank with you, had we killed all of them, the 10.3 million, I would be happy to say, all right, we managed to destroy an enemy. I shall leap into my grave laughing, because the feeling that I have the deaths of five million people on my conscience will be for me a source of extraordinary satisfaction."

He expressed no shame and certainly no remorse. For this reason alone, we must continue to teach our children about the Holocaust and understand the dangerous ramifications of prejudice and racism.

Each story is unique and has a person behind it: a mother, a father, a family, and a thirst for living. Why did some people survive while others perished? What gave some individuals the strength and determination to live while other lives were rapidly taken away? Did luck, smarts, belief in religion, or G-d save them? Every survivor's past has a different purpose and heritage that must be stored in our hearts forever. No human experience is unworthy of analysis. Each man stood alone and struggled for his survival that was reduced to a primordial existence. By addressing these inquiries, hopefully, we will prevent this from reoccurring.

The issue of Jewish resistance taking place during the Holocaust has frequently been challenged. Did Jews go like sheep to the slaughter or did they display acts of resistance? I defy anyone who reads this book to deny that Jews did indeed fight back, under the most excruciating circumstances and unbearable conditions.

People who have heard my uncle's story often ask, "How was he able to live so long in the camps? How was it humanly possible that he could physically survive all the beatings?"

Not many witnesses of the early days of Auschwitz survived to tell their stories. Only a handful of people survived almost six years in concentration camps under the Nazi regime. When American doctors later examined Murray, they said he should have died many times. Why didn't he die?

I certainly don't know the answer. My uncle's greatest strength was his perseverance. He fought for what he cherished the most—life. He was determined to live and tell the world his story with the hope that people would know it *did* happen just the way he and other survivors have told it.

This book is the journey of Murray Scheinberg, my Jewish uncle, from his early life in peaceful Warsaw, Poland, to his imprisonment in two prisons, three concentration camps, a death camp, failed escape attempts, and finally, an unimaginable escape from Dachau. He lived under the Nazi regime from December 3, 1939 until April 29, 1945. He was first arrested and imprisoned on December 3, 1939, as a Polish political prisoner. He was sent by the *Sicherheitspolizei* [German Security Police] to Auschwitz on the first mass transport from Tarnow, Poland, on June 14, 1940, along with approximately 727 other prisoners. He and seven other Polish prisoners successfully concealed their Jewish identity from the Nazis. My uncle was one of the first eight Jews to be imprisoned in Auschwitz, although he was initially registered as a political prisoner and not as a Jew.

Using his wits, strengths, language skills, and probably lots of good luck, after living under the Nazi regime for a deadly five and a half years, he miraculously escaped. Surprisingly, he gained his freedom through shocking events nobody would have expected.

What distinguishes my uncle's story from others? My uncle's story is unique in that he was literally *the first one in and the last one out* of the concentration camps.

As a young child, my parents, my two brothers, Sheldon and Alan, and I visited my Uncle Murray and his wife, Aunt Rose, in California, several times a year. During each visit, our uncle obsessively recounted the horrors he experienced in Europe. He displayed no inhibitions and spared no details in showing us his distorted blemishes throughout his body: scars on his scalp from being severely beaten, crooked fingers from broken bones, and ugly wounds carved throughout his torso. He relived dramatic accounts, retelling them in several languages, violently waving his arms in the air and angrily displaying his tattooed left arm to us—number 31321.

He underwent torture that my brothers and I could not identify with. As Jewish children growing up in upper-middle-class suburbia, we couldn't relate to his accounts of unforgettable pain he endured; starvation, deprivation, mass killings, gas chambers, and beatings. If the three of us, raised by highly educated parents in a pro-Jewish/Zionist environment, responded with relative indifference, how many other people reacted in a similar fashion—especially younger generations? How many other people chose to look the other way rather than face the dreadful truth? And how many people really believed these seemingly impossible stories?

As you turn these pages, you will become immersed in the soul of a brave and remarkable Polish Jew who refused to die. Much of my uncle's story is disturbing and shocking and might be difficult to read. I deliberately did not censor or curtail any of the horrific events, as I wanted it told the way it happened. I hope the reader can look past the suffering and appreciate the heroism and courage behind my uncle's quest to survive.

Preface

First One In, Last One Out is based on the following sources of information:

1. My uncle's recollections, which he shared with my family throughout the years.
2. His written journal.
3. His oral testimonies given to the Simon Wiesenthal Center in Los Angeles, California, on March 4 and March 22, 1988.
4. His oral testimonies given to the USC Shoah Foundation on February 5, 1996.
5. Documents obtained from the United States Holocaust Memorial Museum in Washington, DC.

My mother, an accomplished author, attempted to publish my uncle's memoir in the early 1960s. She had a publisher who was extremely interested in publishing it and proposed a contract.

However, at the last minute, the publisher rescinded the offer with the excuse, "I don't believe the story. This couldn't have happened. Nobody, not even the Nazis, could have done these terrible things, and certainly, nobody could have experienced what your uncle did and survived."

As a result, my mother's manuscript was laid to rest.

The truth was, sadly, in the 1960s the world wasn't ready to bear witness to graphic memoirs of this magnitude. Americans had other concerns and had no desire to hear about the *Shoah*—the Holocaust. The Cold War, Fidel Castro in Cuba, and events in the Middle East and Korea all took precedence over survivors sharing painful memories of Holocaust years.

Having become a Holocaust educator, I decided to pick up where my mother left off. I am not a practiced writer, nor do I pretend to be one. However, a Holocaust survivor's memoir does not need to be written by a professional writer. It needs to be written from the heart, connecting the voice of the survivor to the historical events and providing text to create proof to the world that the atrocities, regardless of how difficult to fathom, did indeed take place. And that is what I, hopefully, accomplished.

During one visit with my uncle, we went to a local park where he played chess with his fellow survivor friends. None of them broached the subject of the Holocaust despite the fact they all had their numbers clearly etched in their arms, identifying their common background. On one occasion, my uncle started to mention an incident that occurred at Auschwitz and was reminded by one of his friends, "We don't talk about that. The past remains in the past."

I recall my uncle's response. "The past can't remain in the past. It is what influences the present and the future."

In a letter my uncle sent to my mother on May 16, 1994, he wrote:

"I was kept alive by many miracles. I don't know how or why. I was a hero to many people whom I kept alive by giving them extra food I stole. I had one goal—to live and help as many people as I could to live. I did what I thought was right. I was named Moishe by my Jewish parents, Moniek by my Warsaw friends, Mondig by the Germans, number 31321 by the guards in Auschwitz, Morris on the ship to America, and now in the United States, I am called Murray. My life took many twists. I was born in Warsaw, Poland, on July 11, 1911. I DIED on December 3, 1939, when German Nazis stole my life and stripped me of my identity and well-being. I was reborn at Dachau on April 29, 1945, by American soldiers, whom I will forever be grateful to. I hope nobody ever has to go through anything near what I did. God bless America."

On his deathbed, my uncle reminded my mother of the manuscript she had started to write years earlier. He begged her to finish it. He still wanted to scream his story to the entire world—somehow, someday. That day is today. My dear uncle, here is your story—your legacy, for the world to hear.

CHAPTER 1
Life or Death

It was April 27, 1945. The night was still. Not a sound could be heard. The abandoned farmland was on the outskirts of Dachau concentration camp, several miles northwest of Munich, Germany. If one didn't know that Germany was at war, one would think the surroundings were peaceful and beautiful. A ditch was concealed from human eyes, and unbeknownst to the Nazis, Mondig lay silently buried in it, with barely enough room to move. The ditch itself was probably no more than five feet deep, three feet long, and two feet wide.

Ten days earlier, Mondig and Rudy feverishly cut through a barb-wire fence at the entrance to the farm,

ignoring the clearly written warning sign in German—
Eintritt Verboten [Entry Forbidden].

The SS guards (elite guards of the Nazis) certainly
knew that Mondig had escaped the camp, and were
undoubtedly actively searching for him with snarling
dogs and rifles in hand. Mondig and Rudy dug feverishly throughout the night to avoid detection. If caught,
they would both be shot on the spot, no questions
asked—Mondig because he was an escaped Jew and
Rudy because he was a Nazi officer assisting a Jew. It
was an unimaginable situation.

After they dug as deep as they could, Mondig slipped
into the ditch and tried to maneuver into a somewhat
upright position, leaning against the side of the ditch.
Rudy had assured him that he would return every night
after his shift at the camp and would alert Mondig of
his arrival by whistling three times. The whistle would
be their secret code.

Mondig spent days and nights in a crouched
position on the hardened dirt, occasionally dozing off
for short periods of time. It was hardly a comfortable
living arrangement, but as it was a matter of life and

death, it was more than acceptable for the time being. Considering all the hardships that Mondig had already endured for the past five and a half years, this seemed relatively easy and was his last possible glimmer of hope for survival. Thanks to Mondig's German Nazi friend, Rudy, he was offered this *safe haven* with the hope that he would be rescued and survive this hellish nightmare.

Who would have ever imagined a German Nazi would come to my rescue? Who would have thought that a Nazi could show compassion?

Barren twigs and overgrown weeds concealed the ditch. From a distance, the ditch appeared to blend into the landscape; no one would suspect that anyone was hiding there. Besides, who would even think of looking in a covered ditch for an escaped Jewish prisoner? Prisoners were not expected to escape from Dachau because of its formidable security. It was against all odds.

The original plan was that this arrangement would last for only several nights until Rudy could find a better hiding place, but Mondig surmised that he must have been there close to two weeks. To Mondig's dismay, Rudy was unable to find an alternative solution. Mondig had no way of determining the exact time or what day it was other than by notches he made on the sides of the dirt walls. When he thought it was evening, he made a notch in the dirt to show a day had gone by, hopefully bringing him one day closer to his freedom.

The ditch was pitch black; not a trace of light came through the twigs. His eyes burned from lack of light. His body was stiff and ached all over. There was no room to stretch or move about. A putrid stench of urine, feces, and perspiration filled the ditch. Almost six years ago, when this nightmare first began, Mondig had a full head of blond hair, but now only strands of gray were visible. He probably lost over 75 pounds. In addition, his once military-looking physique had deteriorated into a frail, ghastly looking skeleton. Yet, remarkably, he was still alive.

Every night, Mondig's heart raced when he heard the three short whistles alerting him that Rudy was near. Rudy, in his neatly pressed Nazi uniform, cleared the twigs off the opening of the ditch and extended his hand to assist Mondig in climbing out of the ditch for fresh air and food. Each movement caused additional pain, and he felt as if his body would shatter into thousands of pieces. However, he had come too far to give up now. He was determined to beat the Nazis and tell the world what they had done. He was going to survive. *Who would believe that humans can inflict such evil on one another?*

Mondig had the routine mastered. After Rudy helped him out of the ditch, Mondig would dust the dirt off the stolen Nazi uniform that he was wearing. He would stretch his cramped legs and breathe fresh air. The air brushing against his face was a gift. It reminded him that fresh air could feel and smell so wonderful.

The two men sat under a nearby tree and ate whatever Rudy could sneak out of his house. Rudy's family would be suspicious if they saw Rudy take food out of the house in the middle of the night. Everything Rudy brought was delicious—what a difference from camp food. Mondig attentively listened to Rudy's reports of the latest news, such as the Soviet Union troops advancing into Poland, the Americans entering Germany, and Germany's weakening military position. The few moments together provided great relief. Rudy's visit not only meant fresh air and food, but also provided Mondig with companionship and the opportunity to converse with another human being without having a gun pointed at him. They were peaceful moments—something Mondig had forgotten existed. Rudy and Mondig shared intimate secrets and established a profound but extremely odd friendship between a Polish Jew and a German Nazi officer.

They enjoyed the nightly conversations. "Life was great in Warsaw. I had a prosperous business, lots of friends, and a good family," Mondig spoke openly to Rudy.

"I didn't have many friends. I was a loner. My father was a soldier, and most of my life was spent hearing his military stories," responded Rudy.

"When did you first hear about Hitler?"

"I can't remember exactly when, but I do recall my dad coming home one day telling us the Jews were responsible for Germany's bad economic state. He told us to stay away from them. I didn't understand how an entire race could be held accountable for Germany's demise, but I wouldn't dare question him. My mother never spoke about Hitler. She was subservient and catered to my dad's beck and call. I was sent to the

Hitler Youth Group as a child. It was always taken for granted that I would follow my father's footsteps, which is what I did."

"Why did you become friends with me, a Jew?"

"When I met you, I didn't think of you as Jewish. You were brave. I had heard rumors that you were in the camp for a very long time. I admired you for being so courageous."

"What do you think Hitler would do if he saw us talking together—a Jew and a German?"

"That's easy to answer. He would surely shoot both of us."

"Who would he shoot first?"

"Let's see. He would probably shoot both of us with the same bullet."

Mondig and Rudy laughed. It felt good to be able to laugh at a time like this.

During his visits with Rudy, Mondig stared at the tranquil sky, wondering if he would ever be able to walk freely.

Mondig thought, *How can the sky be so serene when the world is so ugly? Doesn't G-d know how bad it is down here?*

Although he felt subhuman, he never gave up hope of surviving and seeing his family again.

Initially, Mondig didn't object to hiding in a ditch, but it became more difficult as the days passed. Despite what he was feeling, he never complained to Rudy. He was forever grateful to Rudy for the risk he took in hiding him.

* * *

One night as Mondig waited for Rudy's secret code— the three whistles—Mondig thought it took Rudy much longer than usual.

Something serious must have happened to Rudy. Where is he? Mondig asked himself, panicking, afraid to consider possible explanations.

If Rudy deserts me, I'll be in deep trouble. I'll never make it on my own. I'll be doomed. How can I get out of here alone? Where will I go? What will I do?

Mondig knew that at this point, his body could not withstand any more torture. He felt his days were numbered. He was relying on Rudy to save him.

Life or Death

Seems strange that my rescue lies in the hands of a German Nazi, puzzling as it sounds. How did I ever manage to befriend a Nazi? And how is it possible that a Nazi befriended me? Why did Rudy, my presumed enemy, develop an unusual fondness for me?

Mondig tried desperately to turn around and shift his position, but there was not enough room in the hole to maneuver even his emaciated body. His left leg had fallen asleep, and his back felt as if it was on fire. His entire body was covered with red, swollen bumps and itched from a multitude of insect bites. His left arm was bleeding. He slowly took a few deep breaths to ease his anxiety.

Convinced that something had happened to Rudy, he began to tremble, and his hands started to perspire profusely. Beads of sweat covered his brow. His heart raced. Rudy was never late in his visits.

I can't wait any longer. I must take a chance. I hope and pray I can get out of here. I know I can do it. I've been through much worse.

As he tried to inch his way out, he kept slipping back into the ditch, and he lost his balance. He had no strength left. His body couldn't do what his brain wanted it to do.

9

Just as he was losing hope, he heard the welcoming three whistles. *Whew! Thank goodness. Thank you. Thank you. I knew you would come!* Mondig let out a deep sigh of relief. He was truly ecstatic to see Rudy. Rudy hadn't abandoned him after all. Mondig got out of the ditch with Rudy's assistance, and they hugged and sat in their usual spot.

* * *

Rudy seemed more serious than ever.

"Rudy, why are you late? I know you would only be late if you had a good reason. Is something wrong? Are you OK? Am I going to die?" Mondig inquired nervously.

Rudy quickly replied, "No, Mondig. You are not going to die. At least not in the near future. I am sorry I was late, but I couldn't leave my house. The SS guards called an emergency meeting. I have good and bad news for you. The good news is that the Allies are rapidly approaching Germany. You and I will be switching roles. Now I will be on the run, and you will be rescued. The bad news is that, sadly, this is the last time we will see each other. The Americans are only a few kilometers from here. Our commandant advised us to get out of town. The Allies will be searching for me and the other Nazis. You will be a free man, and ironically, I will be a fugitive."

Mondig's heart skipped a beat, and he was shell-shocked for a few seconds.

Can this be true? Is the war really over? This can't be real. Rudy can't be serious. What does it mean to be free? Will I be able to sleep in a bed with a mattress and eat real food? Will I be able to walk down the street without having a gun pointed at me? Will I see my family again? I must be dreaming.

"You are one of the oldest men in Dachau. You have outsmarted many Nazis. You believed in yourself and never gave up hope. You deserve your freedom. I am happy for you," Rudy told Mondig.

Mondig was dazzled. The idea of being a free man after almost six years of being a prisoner was difficult to imagine. He couldn't fathom what life would be like without the harsh treatment he suffered for so long.

No roll calls? No beatings? No torture? No wondering if I will survive another day?

11

Mondig had waited almost six hard years for this moment. Almost six years of torture and pure hell, being tormented every minute of every day. No words could describe what he had endured—physically and mentally.

For some reason that he couldn't define, he started reciting the Jewish prayer, "*Shema Yisrael, Adonai Eloheinu, Adonai Ehad.*" [Hear O Israel, the Lord our G-d, the Lord is One.]

And then his thoughts shifted to his friend, Rudy. Deeply concerned, he asked Rudy, "What will happen to you, Rudy, my friend? Where will you go? Please don't leave. Stay with me. I will tell the Americans you saved my life. We have come so far together. We are best friends, and friends must stay together. We will start a new life together. Please stay."

"Mondig, as much as I would like to stay with you, you know that's impossible. I have a family I must take care of. I will miss you very much and will always think about you. I will miss our conversations and time together. You have taught me so much, and I am grateful to you."

"How can I ever thank you for what you did for me? I would have never survived without you. You are my true hero—my good friend."

"I wish I could have done more. I regret you had to hide in a ditch for so long. I had hoped to find a better hiding place for you. Trust me, I tried, but I couldn't find another option," Rudy said apologetically.

"Rudy, don't apologize to me! You saved my life. If it weren't for you, I would probably be dead. I am very grateful for everything you have done for me."

Rudy gave Mondig extra food during that final visit, not knowing exactly when the Americans would arrive. Mondig reached in his sock and took out a bag of diamonds he had taken with him from Dachau. Rudy was shocked. "Where did you get these?"

Mondig told him about the time he recognized a woman at the selection platform in Birkenau and how she gave them to him before she was directed to the gas chambers.

Rudy was dumbfounded. "I could never put anything past you, Mondig. You are a master." They both chuckled.

Rudy took the diamonds, caressed them and held them for a few seconds only to say, "Mondig, let's split them. You take half. You will need them to get started in your new life." And they divided the diamonds between them.

Mondig and Rudy knew that the bond between them—a Polish Jew and a German Nazi—was unique and powerful; one never to be forgotten.

However, they had no choice but to say their final farewells. Maybe in a different time and place, their friendship could have continued, but not in Germany and certainly not in 1945. They warmly embraced for a few minutes, not wanting to let go of each other.

With much trepidation, Mondig assumed his uncomfortable but familiar position in his hiding place, and Rudy covered him, although this time Rudy left part of it open so the Americans could find him. Rudy leaned over the partially concealed ditch, and in an emotionally shaken voice said, "Goodbye, my friend. Stay safe. I will never forget you."

As the tears continued to roll down both their cheeks uncontrollably, Rudy proclaimed, *"Auf wierdersehn."* [Goodbye.]

Mondig responded likewise but in Yiddish. *"Biz mir trefn vider, meyn fraynd."* "Until we meet again, my friend."

With those sentimental final words, Rudy disappeared—only to be a distant figure of the past.

* * *

How ironic is it that my last friend is a German Nazi?

Mondig could have never imagined this would happen. It was totally unheard of but for whatever reason, they became friends.

Although delighted with the prospect of being liberated, Mondig felt profoundly sad over Rudy's departure. He wanted Rudy to stay even though he knew it was impossible. Rudy would always have a special place in Mondig's heart.

And then his thoughts returned to his own predicament.

After all I've been through, I can't be caught now.

Mondig was scared. This was the first time he was truly alone.

How long will it take for the Allies to get here? Maybe Rudy was wrong. Maybe they aren't coming after all. What if the Germans overpower them? How long can I survive in this ditch without water or food?

Mondig's head began to spin violently. His heart pounded as he thought, *What did I ever do to deserve this, hiding like an animal under the ground in a ditch, eating only once a day, urinating all over myself, insects biting me, and barely being able to move? Is this living? Will I ever get out of here?*

These thoughts continued to race through his mind. He struggled to catch his breath.

Me, Mondig Scheinberg, a Polish soldier, a highly successful businessman, prominent Polish citizen, married with two wonderful children, having spent almost six years in two prisons, three concentration camps, and one death camp. How is this humanly possible?

Panicking, Mondig called out, "Rudy, Help me! Come back!"

Mondig's frail body collapsed. As he entered a semiconscious state, his mind drifted back to his early life in Warsaw, Poland.

CHAPTER 2

Growing Up in
Warsaw, Poland
—Early 20th Century

Born as Moishe on July 11, 1911, to Yosel and Hannah Scheinberg, he was the youngest of nine siblings; six brothers (David, Aaron, Harry, Motel, Avraham, and Yakov) and two sisters (Ruth and Sarah). They lived in a sprawling, five-room apartment on the fourth floor of a luxury building located in a densely populated Jewish community of Warsaw, Poland.

From Moishe's bedroom, he had a beautiful view of a tree-lined street with a playground where children could always be seen playing. The immediate surroundings contained a children's hospital and a Jewish Community Center, which housed a school, a nursery, and a Judaica library. Warsaw was a thriving Jewish community with newspapers published in Yiddish, Polish, and Hebrew. Life was extremely prosperous for the Jews, and most of Europe's Jews resided in Poland at the time. Jews in Warsaw were primarily professionals: doctors, artists, scientists, and writers, who spoke Yiddish among themselves. Although many Jewish families didn't venture outside of the Jewish community, Moishe's family did. They lived in harmony with all the neighbors, both inside the Jewish community and in the neighboring non-Jewish areas. They never expressed a fear of Warsaw being unsafe for Jews. In fact, Moishe's religion never was an issue. Although he and his family didn't hide the fact that they were Jewish, they didn't publicize it either. In their minds, people were people. Moishe's family had many friends in Warsaw, and their home was frequently the center for entertainment and gatherings.

When Moishe was only four years old, his father was drafted into the Polish army, where he became the conductor of the Polish army band. Moishe missed his father tremendously, and it was very difficult for his mother, Hannah, to raise the children by herself. But she was a proud woman and refused to ask for help from family or friends.

Hannah died two years after his father was drafted, and Moishe was devastated. He had become extremely close with his mother in his father's absence. Luckily, soon after, his father was discharged from the army and returned home. Moishe's father knew he needed to earn a living to give his family the quality of life he wanted for them. He opened a men's designer-clothing business on Twarda Street. He sold to everyone— not just Jews. He was a shrewd businessman and became very successful and wealthy.

As a child growing up in Warsaw, Moishe was very popular and had many friends. Moishe was raised to respect everyone and not judge a person by his or her religion. Moishe's closest friends were Christians—Jozef and Henryk. They were often referred to as the "threesome."

Moishe's father required him to attend *Heder* [Hebrew school] after attending a full day at public school. His father wanted him to have a Jewish background and an understanding of Jewish traditions. Moishe resented having to go to Hebrew school when his two best friends were able to go to the park after school. At 10 years old, he decided to skip Hebrew school without telling his father. He came home from public school and pretended to leave for Hebrew school as usual. Instead, he went to the park and met his friends.

"Hi, Jozef. Hi, Henryk. I'm here to join you," Moishe joyfully announced. Although he felt guilty for deceiving his father, he was happy to be with his friends.

"We are thrilled you are here, but what happened to Hebrew school, Moniek?" asked Jozef. His friends had given him the nickname Moniek, which would someday help conceal his Jewish identity. (The traditional Jewish name, Moishe, would instantly reveal his religion.)

"Didn't feel like going. Let's race to the water fountain. I bet I'll beat you," Moniek responded with a challenge.

Moniek loved the feeling of being in control and missing Hebrew school. He loved it so much that he continued with illicit absences. However, his teacher finally caught on and called his home to find out if he was ill. His father was furious when he discovered what Moniek had been doing.

"Moniek, how can you lie to me and pretend you are in Hebrew school and go to the park instead? Don't you know how important education is? You are a smart boy. Use your brain. It will get you far in life," his father preached to him. He tried to explain the importance of education to his son and at the same time admonished Moniek for deceiving him.

Moniek reluctantly returned to Hebrew school, but every few weeks, he decided to take a risk and skip classes again. Although he didn't like to defy his father, he preferred to be outdoors playing with his friends.

To his father's delight, he was *Bar Mitzvahed* at the age of 13, a Jewish tradition. He was called to the *bimah* [podium of the synagogue], and he flawlessly chanted the *Haftorah* [the reading following the Torah portion]. As the Jewish religion requires, it was now time for Moniek to adhere to his obligation in fulfilling the Torah's commandments. His father proudly gave him his gold watch as a gift. The special family gift had been passed down through the generations, and Moniek would cherish it forever.

Moniek's family considered themselves modern orthodox by today's standards. Although Moniek's father personally never experienced anti-Semitism, he knew the Poles did not admire the Jews. In fact, he had heard about Minister Slathofski, who visited college campuses to advise non-Jewish students not to sit next to Jewish students. The minister spread anti-Jewish propaganda throughout the campuses, describing Jews as swindlers. Moniek's father wanted Moniek to be able to stand up to people like Minister Slathofski who might cross his path in the future.

Several years passed. Moniek's father remarried a woman named Manya. By then, Moniek's father's clothing business was thriving. Moniek spent a great deal of time in the store, knowing that eventually he would take over the business. Moniek enjoyed learning the trade and meeting prestigious customers from all parts of Poland. Moniek sat with them for hours and socialized. The customers loved him, and he loved the attention and the sense of importance, compensating for the neglect he sometimes felt in a family of nine children. He didn't know at the time, but the interactions at the clothing store helped him acquire survival skills that would benefit him in the years to come. He met people who spoke different languages, had different needs, and contrasting personalities. In the business world, he learned to negotiate and cajole, not to mention that he learned the importance of money and the secret magic it possessed.

Moniek's father kept abreast of politics, although it was never discussed openly with his family. He was aware of what was beginning to transpire in Eastern Europe, and he was well informed about the National Socialist Worker's Party in Germany. However, he rationalized that this would pass and that it was of no major significance to him or his family. It was more a conversation piece at the synagogue after Friday night services.

One evening after dinner, Moniek's family heard on the battery-operated radio about Adolf Hitler and his attempted coup d'état, which came to be known as the Beer Hall Putsch. The story piqued Moniek's interest, and he was anxious to hear further information. He was studying World War I in school and knew about Germany's defeat and the humiliation the nation felt with the signing of the Treaty of Versailles.

In reality, the Treaty of Versailles probably contributed to giving Hitler ammunition and setting the breeding grounds for his future despicable actions against the Jews. The treaty devastated Germany. The German-occupied land was reduced tremendously. People's savings were wiped out by hyperinflation. Germany was required to pay large reparations to France and Great Britain for damages incurred during the war. Not surprisingly, the economy of Germany plummeted, leaving many people poor and homeless, without any means of supporting themselves. The *Reichsmark* [German currency] became worthless. Unemployment, chaos and unrest stalked Germany. People felt helpless and had no place to turn. Hitler was handed an excuse to persecute the Jews—blaming the Jews for the crisis Germany was experiencing.

By 1935, Hitler openly defied the treaty, built new airpower, and sent troops to the Rhineland. Great Britain and France ignored Hitler's advances, claiming that he was merely capturing land that previously belonged to Germany.

At the same time, Japan and Italy were also threatening world peace. Japan invaded China, and Italy invaded Abyssinia (Ethiopia). Great Britain, France, and the United States idly watched, concerned about their own domestic problems. They, too, were shattered from the devastation of World War I and were traumatized from their own casualties. Therefore, they favored a policy of isolation with the hopes of not engaging in another war.

The BBC broadcastings of the situation in Germany started to alarm Moniek's family and others. However, as disconcerting as this was, Moniek and his family had a more personal and urgent crisis to deal with. Moniek's father had developed a deep, persistent, hacking cough. He lost his appetite and energy. He stayed in bed all day, barely able to move.

"It's only a slight cough. I'll be fine in a few days," his father whispered, attempting to reassure his family, although they knew better.

Everyone chipped in and tried to nurse him back to health. Moniek's sister gave him tea and hot soup, while Moniek constantly put cool compresses on his forehead. His children held his hand and sang to him. The love of his family circled him. However, despite the nurturing care and constant attention, his fever continued to spike. As his illness progressed, he no longer spoke logically; his words slurred, his breaths became shallow, and his eyes revealed a near lifeless state. The family physician confirmed their suspicion—the end was imminent. The family recited the *Mi Shebeirach* [Jewish prayer for the ill], praying for a miracle, while frantically pacing back and forth. The siblings took shifts so someone was always at his bedside. And then sadly, but as anticipated, he passed away peacefully with his family surrounding him and their love embracing him.

With an empty heart, Moniek led the family in the mourner's *Kaddish* prayer, *"Yitgadal veyitkadash shemeh raba…"*

Moniek didn't have enough time to digest his father's passing before his grandfather unexpectedly passed away. Moniek believed he died of a broken heart, having lost his son. Again, Moniek's family recited the *Kaddish* prayer.

With the passing of both patriarchs, new routines had to be established. His siblings moved out of the house and started to build lives of their own. Moniek became the sole owner of the clothing business with all the responsibilities that came along with it. He was merely 17 years old and probably the youngest businessman in Warsaw, but he was strong and feisty and knew the business. He was determined to succeed and worked long hours while his friends were out having a good time. He knew that through this small sacrifice, the business would afford him wealth in the future. He wanted to be wealthy, enjoy the luxuries of life, and keep the business a family legacy.

Jozef and Henryk stopped by the store frequently and helped with the customers. Moniek rewarded them generously. After a long day at work, the three of them would frequently go out for a drink. Moniek was grateful for the support they gave him at a difficult time in his life.

At 18 years old, he was drafted into the Polish Cavalry, where he proudly served his country for two years. He was a strikingly handsome, robust, muscular young adult who didn't resemble the Jewish stereotype. He had long blond hair and blue eyes—typical, beautiful Aryan features, which were to his advantage. He was treated with respect and dignity in the army and was never diminished as a Jew. He was a loyal, committed Polish soldier with an allegiance to his country, and he achieved a high military rank.

CHAPTER 3

Moniek Faces
Anti-Semitism

While Moniek served his country, his oldest brother ran the business. He was not as swift as Moniek and looked forward to returning the business to Moniek after Moniek's release from the army. Moniek was the shrewd business-man of the family. He was the one surely to succeed.

During one of Moniek's furloughs, he met with his longtime companions, Jozef and Henryk. They strolled in the park and reminisced about their childhood. Out of nowhere, they heard a sharp, piercing shriek. They looked in the direction of the sound. They were shocked at what they witnessed.

"Look," Henryk alerted his friends. "Those boys are harassing a woman and are trying to steal her baby carriage. We have to help her." Moniek quickly agreed. "Let's go." The three friends, all clad in neatly pressed Polish military uniforms, with their guns in their holsters, ran toward the gang. Six teenagers had already surrounded the woman and were screaming obscenities at her while trying to knock over the baby stroller with the baby inside it.

"You *Jude* swine. You shouldn't be walking on these streets. Go back to where you came from. You smell. You are dirtying our streets."

"*Prezestan!* [Stop!] What are you doing?" Moniek screamed emphatically as his two comrades began to reach for their weapons.

The stockiest teenager stared at Moniek and informed him, "In case you can't tell, this woman is a Jew. We don't want Jews here. They are dirty. They will steal from us. Help us get rid of her."

Obviously, they didn't know Moniek was Jewish.

Moniek was not going to reason with the hoodlums. "You are disgusting. Don't you ever talk to anyone like that. Get out of here before we kill you."

The leader of the gang knew the soldiers were sincere in their threat, and the sight of the guns told him it was time to run.

The six boys sprinted away as Moniek reiterated, "If we ever see you again, you will give us good reason to use our guns."

Moniek was becoming more aware of the escalation of anti-Semitism in Poland and the extremes people were taking to foster a hatred of the Jews. This was not a new phenomenon for Jews. However, prior to this incident, he had never personally been confronted with anti-Semitism. At home, in his store, and in the army, people treated him as Polish, no different from anyone else. The vile attack on an innocent Jewish mother shook Moniek up. The woman was minding her own business, merely going for a stroll with her child. It didn't make sense—why would six unprovoked teenagers attack her and make such ridiculous accusations solely because she was Jewish? Moniek was especially sensitive since, after all, despite his "un-Jewish" features and his Christian comrades, he was a proud Jew.

That evening, Moniek remained deeply disturbed by what he witnessed. He blurted out his fears and concerns to his family. He was beginning to pay attention to rumors he heard about the increased anti-Semitism and the harsh treatment of the Jews by the Germans. Hitler promised the Germans a better life if they supported him and eliminated the source of the problem—the Jews! He brainwashed his people into thinking the Jews were the cause of World War I and responsible for the current devastation in Germany. Propaganda spread rapidly and likened Jews to rats spreading disease and causing harm to the German population. "Kill the rats and the disease will stop. Germany will thrive again." Ugly, deceitful words were heard in the streets.

It seemed unimaginable to Moniek that the Germans, or anyone, could even listen to Hitler's gibberish, let alone give him any credence.

How could Jews possibly have caused World War I? Jews served as soldiers for the German motherland. Jews received the Iron Cross award and other medals for valiant service. How can people believe this crazy man—Hitler?

The thought of Jews being the cause of Germany's hardships struck Moniek as absurd, but then again, when people are desperate, they look for a scapegoat. Someone had to be blamed, and in this case, it was the Jews.

Moniek asked Henryk and Jozef if they had heard anything further at their army posts, but they only confirmed what Moniek already knew. The three of them knew that the situation in Germany didn't look promising for the Jews.

The three friends made a pact. "Moniek. We know you are Jewish. However, that has never stood between us. You were, are, and always will be our friend. You are one of us. We will always stick together," assured Henryk.

Jozef added, "Friends forever." With that, the three friends held hands tightly and hugged each other.

Those words comforted Moniek. He also knew that he was well respected within the Warsaw community and was considered an elite citizen. His religious beliefs had not been an obstacle in the past, so why would they be one now? He had friends in the government and knew wealthy businessmen who surely would come to his aid if needed. He convinced himself that he didn't have to be concerned. Moniek was officially discharged from the Polish army in 1931, having achieved the high rank of colonel. He anxiously returned home to an enthusiastic welcoming from his family and friends. He resumed his position as the sole owner of the business, which continued to blossom. Jozef and Henryk were discharged from the army at the same time, and they also celebrated joyously.

Their friendship thrived. Jozef and Henryk were proud of Moniek's accomplishments at the store and enjoyed watching him conduct business with the rich people and hearing him speak so elegantly in many different languages. Moniek had a talent for gabbing and a heart of gold. He treated each customer with dignity and respect. He gave them credit if they were short on money. He never deprived anyone of anything. People came from all over Poland to shop at his store. He had earned a good reputation in the clothing business.

In 1933, the German president, Paul von Hindenburg, invited Adolf Hitler to serve as chancellor of Germany. After von Hindenburg's death, Hitler declared himself the absolute dictator of Germany— the *Führer* [the leader of the country]. At the age of 43, Hitler, an Austrian high school dropout, failed artist, and convicted traitor, became the most powerful man in Europe's greatest industrial state. He was prepared to initiate violence, anti-Semitism, and tyranny across Europe. All civil servants in Germany had to swear an oath of loyalty to Hitler and recite, "Heil Hitler." The Nuremberg Laws were passed on September 15, 1935, at a special meeting at the annual Nuremberg rally of the *Nationalsozialistische Deutsche Arbeiterpartei*, NSDAP (the Nazi party). The first set of laws, the *Law for the Protection of German Blood and German Honor*, forbade marriages and sexual relations between Jews and Germans, while the second set of laws, the *Reich Citizenship Laws*, excluded Jews from citizenship and made race the determining factor in excluding Jews from citizens' rights. Jews were forbidden from entering government-regulated professions such as medicine and education. Jews were forcefully segregated from non-Jews. Jewish children were not permitted to attend public schools. Jews were barred from public theater, beaches, offices, and stores, among other segregation laws. People who violated these laws were imprisoned and sent to Nazi concentration camps.

The rumors kept pouring in of the extreme discrimination German Jews were facing, but it still didn't personally affect Moniek and the Poles in Warsaw, other than an occasional anti-Semitic remark or incident. The major source of information came from the Jews fleeing Germany who were seeking safety with family and friends, although new arrivals from Germany seemed to be decreasing. The Jews who did manage to escape to Poland frantically informed their Polish relatives about Hitler's plan to have a pure, *Judenfrei* [free of Jews] Germany and enlightened their Polish family with the techniques and tactics used in dehumanizing and brutalizing Jews. Hitler wanted his country to be made up of Aryans—the Master Race: blond, blue-eyed, white-skinned Germans. Jews were forcibly being taken away from their homes, never to return. Simply put, life in Germany became unbearable for Jews. Perhaps Moniek was still in denial. Despite the firsthand accounts of dehumanization of the Jews, he held onto the unrealistic hope that he and his family would be safe. And life continued. One afternoon, Henryk entered the store with a beautiful, trim young woman by his side. Moniek immediately noticed her long, shiny black hair and deep-blue sparkling eyes.

He was captivated by her beauty.

"Moniek, I would like to introduce you to my friend, Miriam. She just moved into the neighborhood, and I think you both have a lot in common."

Moniek was enthralled, and it was love at first sight. He saw unbelievable beauty standing in front of him. They began dating steadily and before long were married. They lived in a lovely, sprawling apartment at 11 Welackr Street and had two children; a boy, Pinhas, born in 1935, and a girl, Hannah, born in 1938, whom they named after his mother.

In the meantime, Jozef and Henryk also married, and the three families vowed to have weekly dinners together and maintain their childhood friendship pact. The wives became close friends and all their children played together.

Conversations about Germany's aggression shifted from the dinner tables to the streets. Moniek's circle of friends constantly had fresh updates as to the progress of the German Army, as they attended weekly meetings at the *Pepe*, a very powerful union. They reported to the others about Germany's annexation of Austria on March 12, 1938, which concerned everyone. Even more alarming news came on November 9, 1938, with *Kristallnacht*, or the Night of Broken Glass—the first German government-sanctioned pogrom against the Jews. Herschel Grynszpan, a 17-year-old German-born Jew of Polish ancestry, received news that his family, along with 17,000 other Polish Jews, were deported to Poland. Poland refused to allow them to enter and therefore the Jews were stranded. Herschel's family was able to send word to him about their dilemma.

Seeking revenge, he killed a minor German official, Ernst vom Rath, at the German embassy in Paris. Nazi minister of propaganda Joseph Goebbels used the assassination as an excuse to attack the Jews. The SA (Nazi Storm Troopers) and the Hitler Youth Groups torched 250 synagogues, vandalized 7,000 Jewish businesses, killed almost 100 Jews, and deported 30,000 Jews to Nazi-controlled concentration camps. All of this happened in two days—an unprecedented event. And to top it all, Moniek had heard that the Jews who were the victims of the pogroms and looting were required to clean the streets and pay one billion marks (400 million dollars) in damages to the government.

Moniek and his friends tried to remain optimistic and reassured themselves that they were safe since Germany had a non-aggression pact with Poland. The treaty was created between the Second Polish Republic and Nazi Germany and signed on January 26, 1934. It stipulated that both countries would resolve their differences by negotiations. Additionally, they agreed to relinquish all armed conflict for 10 years.

Surely Hitler would keep his word and adhere to the agreement.

Unfortunately for Moniek and millions of others, he didn't.

CHAPTER 4
Warsaw
Under Siege

Moniek's wife, Miriam, also started hearing frightening rumors at the market. She became fearful of what might happen to the Jews in Poland. Germany and Hitler were the topic of conversation in the street. There was no way to hide from the truth. Anti-Semitism was spreading and Jews were increasingly being persecuted.

Despite it all, Moniek continued to reassure his family, "This will never happen in Poland! We have a strong Polish army and can defend ourselves against the Germans."

Further, Moniek told Miriam and their two children, "And it will never happen to us. We're respectable Polish citizens and have been for generations. My father and I both served in the Polish army. I have a great business, we have plenty of money, and everyone in Poland loves us. I am confident we will be safe here. Don't worry."

"I hope you are right," Miriam responded hesitantly, but in her gut, she sensed he was wrong.

She knew her husband well. He was an optimist and never said a bad word about anyone.

* * *

Conditions in Poland rapidly deteriorated. The non-aggression pact between Germany and Poland didn't seem to hold weight anymore and on September 1, 1939 Germany invaded Poland. World War II had officially begun. Despite all the prior mobilization signs, the attack was a tactical surprise for the Poles. German tanks hounded the Polish artillery and the Poles suffered high casualties. Great Britain and France declared war on Germany on September 3, 1939, while the German forces continued to march deeper into Poland and reached Warsaw.

Moniek heard planes zooming overheard, frightfully close to their home. His children rushed downstairs, panic-stricken, covering their ears. The noise was deafening. This was not an ordinary night. The family huddled together, not knowing what to expect. They saw intense flames rising from the homes across the street. Early in the morning, Moniek turned on the radio and heard the announcer state that bombs and warships had attacked the Polish naval forces in the Baltic Sea. There was heavy shelling in Warsaw. The whistling sound of the airplanes could be heard for miles away. Dishes flew all over Moniek's kitchen. The floor shook, windows rattled, and glass shattered. Pictures fell off the walls. Moniek looked out of the living room window and saw people being dragged from their homes and shot in the street. Hysteria, crying, and gunshots were seen and heard all over the neighborhood. Pandemonium ruled. Moniek's street looked like a mass cemetery with corpses lining the pavement. Buildings were blown up, and people were frantically running for cover. Flames engulfed the surroundings. The odor of heavy smoke permeated, and Moniek placed a handkerchief over his mouth and nose so he wouldn't breath the intense fumes.

Moniek had to react quickly. He grabbed his wife, two children, and a few belongings. He knew of a secure room in the basement of his store. He had to get his family there quickly and safely. Moniek led his family to a secluded path away from the main streets. They ran like rats—fast and furious, staying low to the ground and dodging flying debris and bullets. His neighbors also scrambled for cover. The streets smelled of burned flesh and the feeling of death permeated the area.

Miraculously, they were able to dodge the barrage of bullets and arrived at the store safely. They stayed in a crouched position, without food, for two days before they dared to return home. Extensive fighting continued in the streets, but the Polish army could not withstand the tough German troops. Many Polish soldiers fled. Moniek and his family had no place to go and didn't want to leave their business or home. For so long, he thought they would be safe; he had ignored the rumors he heard. Finally, reality hit home. He could not hide behind the dreadful truth any longer. He was not safe. Nor was his family safe. Warsaw was under siege.

* * *

The fighting intensified and on September 25, otherwise known as "Black Monday", three forts of Warsaw were seized. Several days later, September 28, 1939, after heavy shelling and bombing, Warsaw had no choice but to surrender to Germany. Sections of German-occupied Poland were organized as the General Government while other parts were annexed by the Reich. The radio carried Hitler's speech stating that the conquest of Poland would bring *lebensraum* [living space] for Germans.

"What about us, the Polish people? What is our fate? After all, this is our country," the residents questioned, wondering what the future had in store for them. Their land no longer belonged to them.

The Germans now controlled Warsaw. The years of rumors were no longer just rumors. Moniek and his family now lived in German-occupied Poland! Warsaw was a different city. It was not the Poles' home anymore. Nazi orders intensified. What had happened to the Jews in Germany had come to Poland. Jews could no longer publish newspapers or own radios. They were required to wear an identifying armband with a Jewish star clearly visible. Anyone who was caught disobeying the rules was shot on sight. No exceptions!

With each passing day, life became more unbearable. Moniek tried to maintain a normal lifestyle, hoping to provide some structure and guidance for his family. His close friend Jozef arranged for him and his family to move into an apartment that was outside of the Jewish area to conceal his Jewish identity from the Germans. Although the non-Jewish community of Warsaw knew Moniek was Jewish, nobody revealed his secret. They thought of him as their friend, the local businessman. Also, to his good fortune, his Aryan looks deceived the Germans. As far as Moniek knew, the Germans didn't suspect him of being a Jew, so for the time being, he was safe. After the dust settled, he reopened his store and operated the business the best he could, under the circumstances. He sold clothes cheaply and helped everyone, hoping they, in return, would help him.

Shortly thereafter, a curfew was imposed in Warsaw, and Jews were forced to be in their homes by 7:00 p.m. Still acting as a non-Jew living among non-Jews, this did not affect Moniek, although his children fretted. They were living the good life of an Aryan but didn't know how long it would last.

"Don't worry. Remember, I served in the Polish army, as did your grandfather. Jozef and Henryk will always help us. We are fortunate. We don't look Jewish, and we don't live with the Jews," Moniek reiterated to his family, hoping to put them at ease.

"But what about our Jewish friends?" asked his son, Pinhas. "How can we desert them? Are we being fair to them?"

Pinhas felt guilty leading a double life. He was Jewish and wanted to be with his Jewish friends. Why should he be treated differently? He told his father that he felt as if he was being deceitful to his friends. Moniek tried to explain that things would be better, but the words couldn't come out, as he wasn't sure that was the truth. He, like his son, wrestled with the notion that his fellow Jews were suffering while his family had it relatively easy. But he wanted his family to be safe.

How do you justify to your children that you are concealing your religion so that, hopefully, you and your family will be spared?

Do you scare them and tell them that if you don't keep your religion a secret they might be murdered? Aren't we, as parents, suppose to protect our loved ones?

Moniek repeatedly asked himself these questions.

Moniek knew he had to defend his family. He was a fighter and would do whatever was required. He loved his family and didn't want any harm to come to them.

Several days later, Moniek was walking down the cobblestone streets of Warsaw, as he had done many times. He approached Henryk's house and saw that his friend was in the process of moving boxes from his home. All the furniture was sprawled on the front lawn.

"How are you, Henryk?" Moniek, dumfounded, called out. There was no answer.

"Henryk, did you hear me?" Moniek couldn't imagine that his friend was moving and didn't tell him. It was obvious that Henryk was ignoring him.

Finally, Henryk cautiously approached Moniek and whispered, "Moniek, we can't meet again. I am being forced to move. Things are different now. This is not *our* Warsaw anymore. Jozef helped you get an apartment away from the Jews. You are lucky. You are not like the other Jews. However, we, non-Jews are not permitted to talk to Jews. So far, the Germans don't know you are Jewish. Jozef and I will keep your secret, but I can't jeopardize my own family. If the Germans find out you are Jewish and I am friends with a Jew, they will probably shoot me. They will probably shoot my family as well. I don't like the situation any more than you do. But please understand. I can't take that chance. You must protect your family, and I must protect mine. We can't be friends anymore. I'm sorry. Don't look for me. Be safe. We will meet again... someday... somewhere... somehow."

After years of soccer games, sharing good times, walks, and family dinners, their friendship was doomed. Moniek understood that his friend didn't want to take a chance that the Nazis would discover he was friends with a Jew. He also knew Henryk had to think of his own family first just like he did. However, understanding that didn't help the emotional loss Moniek felt. What happened to the words "friends forever" or the pact they made? Sadly, Moniek went home with an empty feeling.

Although Moniek realized that Henryk had no choice, it bothered him tremendously.

Is that enough of a reason to end a friendship? We were best friends.

Several days later, Moniek discovered the truth as to the reason Henryk was moving—Henryk was living in an area the Nazis had designated as a ghetto for the Jews. The Nazis forced him and other families to evacuate the area so they could get it ready for the Jewish arrivals. They set up the ghetto to segregate the Jews from the non-Jews. It was a major step in persecuting the Jews.

Moniek was truly disturbed over what he perceived was a betrayal of friendship.

* * *

As the restrictions intensified, Jews were no longer allowed to pray in the synagogue. However, on the holiest Jewish holiday of the year, Yom Kippur, Moniek and his circle of Jewish friends were determined to find a way to pray together. The night before Yom Kippur, Jews around the world customarily start their 24-hour fast and ask G-d for forgiveness and atonement for sins they may have committed during the past year. For centuries, Jews gathered in the synagogues to pray during Yom Kippur. The Jews of Warsaw did not even entertain the idea of not continuing their Jewish traditions and denying their obligations to G-d. Moniek had never missed a service on a High Holiday and no German was going to make him miss one now. The only question was how he and his friends were going to pull it off.

However, Moniek had an additional dilemma. Until then, he successfully concealed his religion from the Germans.

What if a Nazi sees me entering the synagogue? My secret will be revealed, and they will surely know I am Jewish. What about my family? What will they do to them?

Putting himself in harm's way was one thing, but his family? Now he sounded like his friend Henryk.

Moniek certainly didn't want to put his family in a dangerous situation, but he also didn't want to relinquish a longtime family tradition and a commitment to G-d. Was this a test?

Do I have to decide between religion, G-d, and my family?
Surely, there is a compromise.

Determined to uphold the Jewish tradition while
still keeping his family safe, he devised a plan with the
rabbi. The plan entailed two young, non-Jewish brothers pretending to talk to each other outside a house.
The rabbi paid the *goyim* [non-Jews] a huge amount
of money to use their house as a makeshift synagogue.
The two boys stood guard as groups of three Jews
dressed as workers snuck into the basement of his
house. If the boys saw a German approaching, they
would signal by singing a German song—their code.
Miraculously, everyone made it in without any incident.
In his sermon, the rabbi spoke of the terrible things
happening—of disappearing Jews, dehumanizing acts
of cruelty, and of further restrictions. He regretfully
announced that several members of the synagogue had
mysteriously disappeared and never returned. Nobody
knew where they went. He did not understand why
this was happening but told everyone to continue to
believe in G-d, and G-d would save them. The services
were abridged, as nobody wanted to press his luck at

this illegal gathering. But they prayed and upheld the tradition the best they could under the circumstances.

Everyone thought G-d would forgive them for the makeshift synagogue and for speeding up the prayers.

Or would He?

CHAPTER 5

The 2:00 a.m.
Knock on the Door

At 2:00 a.m. on December 3, 1939 —a night Moniek would never forget—he was abruptly awakened by a pounding on the front door. Half asleep, he ran downstairs with Miriam following close behind. When he opened the door, he was staring directly at three *Sicherheitsdienst des Reichsführers* [German SD] soldiers dressed in neatly pressed, gray-blue uniforms and brightly polished black boots. The SD was the German security service who concentrated on locating people they believed to be enemies of the state. Behind them, Moniek saw a faint shadow of a fourth man, but it wasn't clear who he was. He was covering his face and avoiding eye contact. When

Moniek got a closer look, he almost fainted. It was Jozef, Moniek's close childhood friend, standing with the German soldiers!

In shock, Moniek asked, "Jozef, what are you doing here at this hour with these soldiers?"

There was silence. Jozef looked at the floor, appearing ashamed, and said nothing. One of the soldiers walked up to Moniek, slapped him on the face, and put his gun firmly against the back of his head. "Why are you talking to him? He is of no concern to you. Look at yourself. You are not even dressed!"

Moniek wanted to laugh. It was the middle of the night. *Why should I be dressed? I was sleeping.*

Moniek thought he was having a nightmare; possibly, he was walking in his sleep.

Why isn't Jozef telling the German to put his gun away? Why is Jozef with them? This can't be happening.

But the cold, hard pistol pushing into the back of his head confirmed to Moniek this was real and that for some strange reason, Jozef was cooperating with the soldiers.

Pinhas, hearing the ruckus, called from his bedroom, "What's happening, Papa?"

"Go back to sleep. Everything will be fine," Moniek lied, trying not to alert his son to their impending danger.

With a gun still pointed at his head, the soldiers ordered Moniek to get dressed and to be ready to leave his house in two minutes. If not, his wife and two children would be shot.

Did they finally discover I am Jewish? Jozef swore he would never reveal my secret.

He recomposed himself and replied, "*Jawohl* [Yes]. I'll be ready in a minute."

He dashed to the bedroom, grabbed whatever clothes he saw first, got dressed, and rushed downstairs. He heard his wife pleading with the soldiers to let her go with him, but they only responded by hitting her in the stomach with a rifle.

"Get the key to your store and follow us. Move! *Schnell* [Quickly]!" ordered the soldier.

Moniek did as ordered, and they pushed him out the front door. He managed to utter his last few words to his family—"I love you."

And with those three words, the tears rolled down

Moniek's face as he shut the door to his house—for the very last time.

* * *

Outside his home, Moniek saw two large jeeps. Two soldiers jumped into the second jeep. The third soldier and Jozef directed Moniek to go to the first jeep. The driver drove through the winding streets as Moniek's former friend, Jozef, guided him directly to Moniek's prominent clothing store. Moniek tried to make eye contact with Jozef, but his "friend" continued to ignore him.

How can he do this to me after all our years of friendship and the pact we made?

The promise of staying together as lifetime friends was apparently a lie.

Henryk had already stopped talking to him, and now it seemed that Jozef was betraying him as well.

When they arrived at Moniek's store, the leader firmly ordered, "Open the door."

Fearful of the consequences, Moniek quickly fumbled

for the keys. His hands shook from fear, but he finally managed to open the door.

"Out of the way!" shouted the leader, as two of the soldiers and Jozef entered the store.

One soldier stayed behind, guarding Moniek. Moniek looked around and saw another truck approaching. It stopped directly beneath the window of the store. Within a few minutes, the soldiers started throwing all the clothing out of the window into the truck.

"Please," Moniek desperately pleaded to deaf ears. "Don't do this!"

Moniek stood helpless, watching clothing—coats, shirts, and belts—being removed.

They ignored his pleas and emptied the entire contents of the store in a relatively short time. All the years of hard work were destroyed in merely a few minutes right before his eyes.

How many years did he and his father put their blood, sweat, and tears into making the store one of the most successful clothing stores in Poland? And now? Moniek stood powerless, watching the destruction of his family legacy. He felt as though a knife were stabbing him in his heart. He grabbed his stomach as he was engulfed with nausea and dizziness. Tears filled his eyes, but he could do nothing. He was at their mercy. If he attempted to fight back, he knew he would be killed instantly.

Once the store was void of merchandise, the soldiers proceeded to destroy the furniture and appliances. And after that was accomplished, the soldiers hurled bricks at the outside windows, smashing the store façade to pieces. The store was in shambles, beyond recognition, destroyed, with all the expensive merchandise scattered in the soldiers' truck.

When the soldiers were pleased with their actions, they forcibly pushed Moniek back into the jeep. He banged his head against the door, causing him to bleed profusely. He was still in such a state of shock that he didn't feel the pain or even notice the bleeding. Shortly thereafter, the jeep jerked forward and started moving.

After catching his breath, Moniek finally mustered up the courage to ask his assailants, "Where are you taking me? What will you do with my family?"

"You are going to the Pawiak police station. You are under arrest. You are a political prisoner."

If it were another era, Moniek would have laughed. He didn't know what being a "political prisoner" meant. He never even attended the meetings his friends went to. He knew nothing more about politics than the average Polish citizen. Sure, he listened to the radio, but so did everyone else. Did that make him a criminal? He had heard of the Pawiak police station but thought it was Warsaw's main prison for Communist Party members. He certainly wasn't a Communist. At the time, he didn't know that the prison had become a German Gestapo prison and was used primarily for interrogation and executions.

Moniek shivered. *What lies ahead for me? What is a political prisoner? Did they arrest me because I am Jewish? Did Jozef disclose my secret?*

CHAPTER 6

Life Changes in a Flash at Pawiak Prison, Poland

It was difficult to comprehend how life could change so drastically in a split second. Only one day earlier, Moniek was a highly successful businessman and owner of the largest men's apparel store in Warsaw, and today he was riding in a jeep to Pawiak prison (later to become the largest political prison in Poland during the Nazi occupation), arrested for a reason unknown to him. How quickly the transformation took place for Moniek. Yet, this was only the beginning of many changes to occur.

What does it mean to be a political prisoner? I am a businessman.

The jeep rumbled through the uneven, cobblestone streets. A large, open truck filled with German soldiers was parked on a corner. Shouts of "Heil Hitler" could be heard everywhere as the jeep made its way to the police station. People saluted the German soldiers marching on the streets. The German swastika flag hung from buildings. The soldiers wore Nazi armbands with a swastika prominently displayed on their sleeves. Moniek was not familiar with this different Poland, and he certainly did not want to be associated with it. He was almost relieved his father was deceased and didn't have to witness this.

* * *

Why am I a political prisoner?

Nobody would answer him.

Moniek tried not to react to what he saw on the streets but rather to his own puzzling situation.

Upon arriving at the prison, the soldiers escorted Moniek into the chambers where a police officer confronted him. A picture of Adolf Hitler hung on the wall, and the Nazi flag filled the corner of the room.

"What have we here?" the officer asked slyly, looking directly at Moniek. The officer ordered, "Empty your pockets, Mondig."

Moniek looked around to see if someone else was in the room. He had never been referred to as Mondig. Seeing he was the only prisoner in the room, he assumed the command was directed at him. Moniek complied, although he laughed to himself. What could be in his pockets? He was forced to get dressed at 2:00 a.m. after being abruptly awakened by soldiers. He didn't have time to plan what he would take. There was nothing in his pockets except for a pen and a handful of coins. The officer was visibly disappointed.

He looked at Moniek again and spotted the gold watch on Moniek's left wrist. "Mondig. What's this? Hm. A very nice gold watch," the officer said, lifting Moniek's hand to display the watch he was wearing. Moniek was not going to question the new name the officer had apparently given him—Mondig.

Is it because the soldier can't pronounce Moniek, doesn't like my name, or doesn't even know my name? Whatever the reason, I have a new name. And a new person emerged—Mondig—although that was the least of his concerns. Mondig was more upset over having to relinquish his watch, his last memorabilia from his deceased father, the watch his father gave him on his joyous *Bar Mitzvah* day. He loved the watch. It was magical. Whenever Mondig looked at it, good memories, peace, and solace would emanate. Not this time.

"Take it off. It is now mine. It will look great on my wrist." The officer beamed.

"Please. Take anything, but not my watch. I will do whatever you want, but let me keep my watch." Mondig knew he could not save his treasured watch. Reluctantly, he complied and surrendered his watch. The officer promptly put it on his wrist, satisfied with his new acquisition.

Mondig tried to digest the day's events. He still had absolutely no clue as to why all this was happening to him and why his best friend betrayed him.

How is it possible that I am standing in a prison staring at a picture of Adolf Hitler?

"Guards," the officer commanded. "Take this prisoner away." Two husky guards quickly appeared from nowhere, grabbed Mondig, and threw him into cell 19, which was already overcrowded. It was built for about 10 men but now held 25. Mondig barely had room to move. He asked the prisoner sitting next to him why he was there, but the inmate wouldn't answer. Nobody would talk. Silence prevailed. One prisoner put his finger to his mouth, advising Mondig to be quiet.

Shortly after Mondig's arrival, a gunshot broke the silence. Mondig peeked through the small window leading to an outdoor passage. He saw a man lying on the ground, covered with blood. Apparently, a soldier had shot him in the head. The sound of a gun would become a familiar sound to Mondig and the other prisoners.

Mondig immediately learned the *survival* rules of the prison, which later proved to be the same rules that governed the camps:

Don't appear too smart, too stupid, or too weak. Don't cry, as crying is a sign of weakness.

Show no anger or self-pity.

Follow orders quickly. Don't argue or complain.

Don't call attention to yourself. Do not display any sign of resistance.

Look healthy. Pinch your cheeks if needed. Befriend a Nazi.

And most of all, never give up hope. Keep the will to survive close to the heart.

Whenever Mondig heard the soldiers call out, *"Ausrichten* [Line up]," he quickly rose and stood at attention. He became a puppet for the Germans' entertainment. One Nazi, who referred to himself as Officer Goodman, would open all the cells, and all 400 male prisoners quickly charged out. The prisoners were ordered to squat and jump like frogs. After they complied with the orders, they were instructed to sing a song while standing on one foot. Officer Goodman laughed while whipping prisoners randomly. About 10 men were ordered to walk on burning coals, and as they did, Officer Goodman shot them. Finally, after amusing the soldiers, the surviving prisoners were permitted to return to the dreary cells. By this time, Mondig could not possibly have imagined what would happen to him next. He had never experienced anything like that. As a Polish soldier himself, he never interrogated anyone with such brutality. He didn't understand how any human being could be so animalistic.

"Why am I here?" Mondig tried asking feverishly. Once again, he heard the same warning.

"Don't ask questions if you want to live. Do as you are told and shut up," a fellow inmate advised.

For the next seven days, Mondig did nothing but participate in the inhumane entertainment games for the soldiers. A popular "sport" involved forcing the prisoners to lie down, lift their legs in the air, and then walk on their backs—an almost impossible feat. The guards laughed as this took place.

After the soldiers tired of the games, Mondig was brought to the interrogation cell and was whipped. The interrogator asked questions, but Mondig had no answers. In fact, Mondig didn't even understand what was being asked. The questions made no sense.

Mondig slept on a wooden floor, curled in a corner of the cell. There were no bathrooms. They were allowed to go to the outhouse once in the morning and once in the evening. Food was sparse, and they were only given leftover food that the Nazis didn't want.

How bad will it get? How can it possibly get worse than this?

CHAPTER 7

Transfer to Tarnow
Prison, Poland

On Mondig's eighth day of imprisonment, December 11, 1939, two guards, one tall and slim and the other rather plump, entered the cell. In a harsh voice, the tall guard yelled, "Mondig."

Mondig immediately stood up and shouted, "Jawohl," identifying himself.

"You will come with us," the guard ordered, leading Mondig to a bench outside of the police station. "Sit here until we are ready for you." Mondig clamored for water. He couldn't remember the last drink he had. He politely asked, but was told, "*Wassertrinken verboten* [Drinking water is forbidden]."

Some prisoners drank their own urine out of desperation to remain hydrated.

It seemed as if hours had passed until finally, in the middle of the night, a soldier approached him and directed him to a jeep parked across the street. There were approximately five jeeps in all. Motorcycles with soldiers holding machine guns straddled each jeep. The soldiers directed Mondig and other inmates to the last jeep.

An officer sat in the back with the prisoners and instructed them, "Don't laugh, don't smile, and don't talk. If you do, you will give me a reason to shoot you." He gave each prisoner one piece of stale bread for the long journey.

The jeep sped through the streets, cutting sharp corners. The streets looked vastly different from the Poland he remembered. The people looked different. German soldiers rode their motorcycles, and Nazi flags bearing the swastika symbol flew from the rooftops. Peddlers and beggars lined the cobblestone sidewalks. They looked hungry and sick. Finally, several hours later, the jeep arrived at its destination: the large prison in Tarnow, 300 kilometers away, in southern Poland.

"Get out," Mondig was ordered.

He jumped from the jeep onto the street below and was forcibly led into a prison cell. He noticed a few Jewish prisoners who displayed the white band with a Star of David around their arms. The non-Jewish prisoners, Mondig learned, were ministers, doctors, or politicians. They didn't seem to know why they were in prison any more than Mondig did. Somehow, the Germans must have felt they were a threat. Mondig still managed to conceal his Jewish identity, so he was not compelled to wear the white Star of David armband. He knew once they were able to take a shower, this would be difficult, as like other Jews, he was circumcised. This was the only time in Mondig's life he was happy not to shower. He wondered how long he could keep his secret.

Mondig estimated that the prison contained approximately 40 small cells, with 12 men in each cell. The handful of Jews were herded into one cell. Non-Jews occupied the others. Most of the prisoners were informed that they were arrested for political crimes. The cells were bare except for a thin, ripped straw mattress on the floor. The stone walls were cold, and the one tiny window in each cell was too high to look out from and too small for sufficient air or light to enter.

"You are a political prisoner," the guard officially informed Mondig as he led him toward a crowded cell designated for Polish political prisoners. He was instructed to wear a red triangular patch on his uniform, identifying his status.

Although Mondig preferred being with the Polish prisoners rather than the Jews, it made no sense to him that he had been arrested at all. And he, like the others, was never given a trial.

How does owning a store classify me as a political prisoner?

One of the officers finally disclosed to him that his "friend", Jozef, turned him in. Jozef was attending an underground political meeting when the police raided it and took him prisoner. Under excruciating interrogation, he succumbed and told the officers that if they stopped beating him, he would show them where they could get rich. Jozef betrayed his childhood friend and told the assailants about Mondig's store and the riches inside. The officers suspended the beatings. They freed Jozef but imprisoned Mondig.

Mondig lost both of his close friends, Jozef and Henryk, to the threats and fears of the Nazis. He wondered at what length he would go to save his own life, not knowing at the time that he, too, would be confronted with similar dilemmas in the near future.

Is deception and thievery permissible if it saves your life? What would G-d say?

Mondig didn't have an answer at the time but would continue to struggle with the moral question in the years to come.

Although angered by the betrayal, he was pleased that at least Jozef didn't inform the authorities that he was Jewish.

Mondig continued to plead with the guard. "I haven't done anything wrong. I don't even know anything about politics. I am a rich man. I will give you whatever you want if you let me go free."

The guard laughed. "Rich? Not anymore." He smashed the butt of his gun against Mondig's right shoulder. "You have nothing to give me. You are poor, like everyone else here."

Mondig's screamed in agonizing pain from the blow and fell to the ground.

"That will teach you." The guard continued to kick Mondig while he forced another prisoner to drag Mondig to his cell.

Later that night, as Mondig tossed and turned on the straw he was sleeping on, still in pain from the harsh blow to his shoulder, a prisoner in his cell screamed uncontrollably, "Let me out. Let me out. I can't take it any longer!" A few minutes passed. The guard in charge approached and let him out. He dragged the screaming man to the end of the corridor. Mondig heard a sharp gunshot. He never saw the man again.

Life in prison was unbearable, although Mondig knew that the Jewish prisoners had it worse. The food—stale bread and coffee for breakfast, soup for lunch and dinner—had no nutritional value and tasted awful. He often found a pebble or a button in his soup. Although hard to believe, this was worse than the first prison. The prisoners slept touching each other. They had no privacy whatsoever. Similar to the first prison, visitors were not permitted, and all news from the outside world was stifled. It was a world that was unfit for humans.

How is my wife, Miriam? How are my children, Pinhas and Hannah? I hope they are not experiencing the torment I am. I hope G-d is watching over them.

Mondig wanted desperately to know the fate of his family but had no means of finding out. He longed to see them, to hug them, and to kiss them.

Mondig approached a younger man in his cell. When the guard was nowhere in sight, Mondig leaned closely to his cellmate and asked, "Do you know how long we will be here?"

The man answered in hushed tones, "I wish I knew, but they didn't tell me anything. It seems that everything is a secret."

At that moment, a guard walked by and overheard them. "No talking," he warned sternly, "or you will be sorry."

* * *

Mondig reminded himself of his *survival rules*. He could not take any unnecessary risks and had to remain cautious at all times. That was the last time Mondig asked questions. He knew he had to rely on his skills to outsmart the enemy. As a Polish soldier, he had learned some military strategies, and he was familiar with the Polish mentality. He spoke English, Yiddish, German, and Polish fluently. He was a strong, muscular man and had an Aryan look with his blond hair and blue eyes. From his business experience, he knew how to assert himself and speak to people. Most importantly, he was courageous. On that day, he swore to himself that he would do his best to live. He would never complain; he would use his smarts and accede to Nazi demands—for the time being. He wanted to breathe fresh air and see his family again.

Time passed slowly. For one hour a day, the prisoners were taken for a walk in the prison yard. "Hands behind your back," the guard in charge ordered as he led the prisoners to the central courtyard.

They marched "left, right, left, right" in a sweeping circle with the guards laughing and mimicking them.

A large opening on the north side of the courtyard overlooked the street. Mondig always tried to steal a glance when the guards weren't looking. One day, he noticed a man walking past a Nazi soldier.

Faintly, he heard the Nazi call out, "*Jude*, take off your hat when you pass me."

Mondig couldn't hear the man's response, but everyone heard the gunshot that followed.

Soon after, Mondig noticed a large truck loaded with skeletal bodies. He instinctively covered his face to hide his reaction and continued to march. A guard noticed Mondig viewing the outside.

"If you insist on looking there, watch what will happen." He beat Mondig over the head with his stick.

Mondig quickly learned another rule. *Do not display facial expressions—maintain a stone face at all times.* Mondig tried to observe everyone's actions and learn what worked best in appeasing the Nazis, though only as a survival mechanism until he had the opportunity to escape.

One night, with the guards asleep, a newly arrived prisoner passed along news from the outside world.

Although the prisoners knew the rule of silence, the prisoner continued talking. The information was spellbinding. Germany had abolished the Free City of Danzig, which was established in 1920 under the protection of the League of Nations, providing Poland access to a seaport. The Nazis incorporated the area into the newly formed Reichsgau of Danzig-West Prussia and sent most of the remaining Jews to concentration camps. The League of Nations was established at the conclusion of World War I with the idea of resolving differences by debate—not by war. Hitler overtly ignored the resolution and implemented his own agenda. The disturbing news added to the already heartbreaking situation.

* * *

Mondig guessed it was a Tuesday. The guards in the prison were apparently becoming bored with their regular daily routines and decided to have some fun with the prisoners. An hour earlier than usual, the guards came and opened the cells.

Mondig learned that the familiar "entertainment games" from Pawiak also took place at Tarnow. "Everybody out! Lie down. Hands high. Now crawl on your stomachs to the courtyard!" the guard barked.

The guards laughed at the spectacle; it was almost impossible to crawl with hands held high. Besides, the weakened prisoners hadn't eaten a decent meal in months. A few men couldn't physically adhere to their commands, and they were pulled out of the line. They were directed to walk normally, but when they reached the outskirts of the courtyard, the guards lined them up against the wall. In full view, a guard shot them, one by one, to set an example for all the prisoners.

The guard shouted to the survivors, "Get up from your stomachs. Take your clothes off."

Mondig had dreaded this moment. How could he conceal his circumcision? It was bitterly cold and snow was falling. Nonetheless, the prisoners followed orders. They removed their prison suits, piled them in a heap, and proceeded to the showers. Mondig managed to cover his genitals with his hands, again keeping his Jewish identity a secret. The water was freezing. One minute later, it became unbearably hot. Then back to cold. And then hot. The soldiers enjoyed teasing the prisoners and seemingly loved watching their torment. Nobody looked at Mondig's body, as they were all in so much pain themselves. Mondig thought he was safe—at least for the time being.

After the shower, the remaining prisoners scrambled for their clothing. "*Nein* [No]," said the guard. "Stand still!"

Again, Mondig's heart raced.

Surely, now someone will discover my identity.

His secret was finally discovered. The shrieks of "*Jude*" could be heard across the prison, with fingers pointing at Mondig.

Mondig was beaten by the other Polish inmates and immediately transferred to the Jewish cell, which consisted of seven Jews. This time he was given a yellow armband to wear.

Prisoners died every hour from illnesses, beatings, and shootings. The cruelty never stopped. The Gestapo played a game among themselves by lining up the Jews and seeing who could kill the most Jews in the least amount of time. The survivors were forced to stand in the cold on one foot for several hours. Mondig could never have imagined how brutal people could be.

How is a human being capable of inflicting so much pain on another person? How is one person able to reduce another to a mere nothing—to deprive him of even the smallest things in life—a picture, a handkerchief, a comb, a mirror?

Mondig was living in a corrupt facility made of evil. Why?

What did all these people do to warrant being treated worse than an animal? Where is G-d when He is needed the most?

Mondig was absorbed in thought, thinking about Miriam and his children. He had no idea if they were safe, but he was determined to reunite with them in the future. Thinking about them gave him the incentive to fight back. He wanted to live and to show the world the cruelties Nazis inflicted on innocent people.

A new prisoner told the others how, in Poland, most Jews were confined to ghettos and frequently transported to *new settlements*, never to return. Stories of beatings in the street were common. Tales of cutting Orthodox men's beards, spitting on religious

Torah parchment, and demanding old ladies scrub the streets were shared among the prisoners when they thought the guards wouldn't hear them.

* * *

Every time a new prisoner arrived, the veterans grilled him. "Do you know my family? What happened to them? What are these concentration camps we hear about?"

On June 14, 1940, six months later, while Mondig was being detained in his cell, he heard an announcement over the loudspeaker. "Mondig, come forward."

Is this good or bad? Mondig was terrified. "*Jawohl.* I am Mondig."

The Germans called out seven other Jewish names. Each of them identified himself.

"Take your belongings. Leave your prison uniform here. You are being transferred to work in a sock factory in Germany. Wait here until we call you. Understand?"

And they waited and waited to be taken to the unknown. Although he didn't know what to expect, Mondig felt his first glimmer of hope in a long time. He was now wearing relatively normal, clean clothes. His Jewish armband slipped off when he took off his uniform. Luckily, the guard didn't notice. Pushing his luck, Mondig conveniently put his Jewish armband in the pile of uniforms, as did the seven other Jewish prisoners. It seemed that this act went undetected, and nobody realized the Jewish prisoners had *conveniently* left behind their Jewish armbands. Mondig hoped that wherever they were going, he wouldn't be identified as a Jew, as he knew the fate of Jews was dismal. Maybe Mondig would be able to keep his secret again.

Is G-d giving me another chance? Maybe he is giving me guidance in standing up to my enemy so I will triumph.

He thought that life couldn't possibly be worse, considering what he had already been through. Work sounded good. It had to be better than being forced to participate in inhumane entertainment games and constantly being tortured.

Mondig would soon find out that, unfortunately, he was wrong.

Until then, he didn't know the true meaning of torture.

Unbeknownst to him at the time, he was about to be one of the first eight Jewish prisoners sent to Auschwitz.

CHAPTER 8

Arrival at Auschwitz Concentration Camp

Mondig and seven other Jews classified as "political" prisoners were forced to march out of the prison with a total of 728 Polish prisoners. (Their Jewish identities were unknown to the Nazi guards at the time.)

The SS yelled at them to walk faster. There was nobody on the streets. Tarnow resembled a ghost town. Upon arrival at the station, they were told, "Any resistance, and you will be punished."

They boarded the truck in the middle of the night. The sky was devoid of stars, and darkness surrounded them. It was completely silent. All "unofficial" eight Jewish prisoners were anxious to leave the prison where they had been confined and brutally tortured for so long. They were all Jewish, but the guards still failed to notice they weren't wearing their Jewish armbands. They hoped that this stroke of good luck would continue because whatever was in store for them would be considerably worse if the guards knew they were Jewish. They had agreed to keep their Jewish identity a secret. Mondig remembered the pact he made with his two non-Jewish childhood friends and hoped that this time the pact would not be broken.

Where is this work place they are taking us? Wherever it is, it can't be as bad as the prison was. Nothing can be as bad.

Mondig didn't know how wrong he could be.

A guard came on the truck and handed each prisoner a thin slice of molded bread with what looked like a slice of ham. "Here's your food for the next three days," the guard told them gruffly.

Mondig's short-lived optimism was soon aborted. The molded bread portended what was in store for them. The truck was small, and on each side, there were low wooden benches. The prisoners sat on one side. Two SS guards with long, thin rifles slung over their shoulders climbed on the opposite bench and faced the eight prisoners. The truck roared off, leaving a trail of dust behind. Mondig was elated to say goodbye to the prison and watched as it appeared smaller and smaller. In a few minutes, it was completely out of sight. Mondig stared at his slice of ham. Although not an ultra-religious man in Warsaw, he always followed the Jewish dietary laws pertaining to pork. He never ate pork, as it is strictly prohibited in Jewish law. Eating non-kosher food in prison was one thing, but somehow eating pork just didn't seem right. He was starving but held onto his beliefs and refused to eat it.

Mondig whispered to his friend Henig, who was next to him, "Do you want my ham?"

"No talking," the SS guard snapped, taking the rifle from his shoulder and pointing it directly at Mondig.

Mondig stiffened but remained calm. He should have known better. He knew the rule of *no talking*.

A few minutes later, when the guards weren't looking, he slipped the piece of ham into Henig's hand. If he wasn't going to eat it, Henig would.

Henig stared at Mondig, and his eyes twinkled with gratitude as he devoured the pork.

The ride was extremely bumpy, and Mondig had to hold on to the bench so he wouldn't fall. He lost all sense of time and had no idea how long they traveled, but it was still dark when they arrived at their destination. The truck made an abrupt stop, and Mondig and his fellow inmates were ordered to get out and stand at attention. There were several other trucks with hundreds of prisoners, although no one was wearing a Jewish armband. People seemed to come from various facets of life: old, young, frail, men, women, and children.

Mondig had never seen so many people gathered together at a central location. They all looked at each other in disbelief—not knowing what to expect.

A loud, firm voice could be heard over the loudspeaker. "You will be boarding a train shortly. You are being sent to a work camp in Germany to work in a factory. If you work hard and do as you are told, you will be treated well and will be discharged soon. If you don't, you will be dealt with accordingly."

This sounded like a plan, and Mondig's spirits were temporarily lifted. He had no complaints about working hard if it would bring him his freedom. Moments passed, and Mondig saw a familiar face. He recognized one of the prisoners as a customer from his former store in Warsaw. Mondig desperately wanted to approach him and inquire about his family, but he knew what the consequences would be if he got caught. He decided to wait and try to sit next to him on the train.

It seemed as though they waited for hours for the train to arrive. As the sun began to rise over the horizon, Mondig saw something that resembled an old, dilapidated cattle car. Mondig surmised that that train wasn't for them. It was for animals. Their train would probably be the next one. Mondig was mistaken.

The cattle car stopped, and the orders followed. "Quickly and quietly get on the train," the SS guard, ordered in German. "*Schneller* [Faster]."

The prisoners were pushed into the cattle car. The SS guards continued pushing everyone into the small cars until they were packed like sardines. There were probably a hundred people in the car with Mondig. They were given one bucket, which they were told was for bathroom purposes. It was placed on the far side of the car. There was only one small window about six inches wide and six inches long, covered with barbed wire, barely providing the prisoners with ventilation and light. The male prisoners took charge and instructed the women and children to stand on the side with the window. Men lifted the small children onto their shoulders to allow for extra floor space. They maximized the limited space allotted to them. The SS guards shut the door, and the prisoners were locked inside like a herd of cattle living in despicable accommodations. In no time, the stench was putrid; the foul odor of urine and feces prevailed. Cries were heard as people lost their senses and collapsed.

Mondig thought about his stay in the prison and convinced himself that since he was capable of enduring the torment there, he could tolerate the vile train ride, although he, like others, hoped the trip would be short. He tried to think of more pleasant times—his family, his beautiful hometown of Warsaw. He knew he had to be strong. Mondig managed to push through the crowds until he located his former customer. He initiated a conversation and asked his old friend what was happening in Warsaw and if he had any news to share about his family. Sadly, his friend informed Mondig that he thought the Germans took his family from their home to an unknown location. It wasn't a good sign, but maybe they were still alive. His friend didn't say they had been murdered. Mondig had known that Jews were sent to live in the Warsaw ghetto. He remembered his friend had to relinquish his home for the Jews. Living conditions were terrible in the ghetto, and people were dying of starvation and diseases, but maybe, somehow, his family had escaped. Mondig needed to hold on to the glimmer of hope that one day he would be reunited with his family. Without that hope and dream, living was pointless.

People engaged in conversation to pass the time and hopefully hear about their loved ones. Those who had the strength to talk would shout out, "Is anyone from—? Does anyone know my family?" Several connections were made.

After a few minutes of depressing dialogue, one woman suggested, "Let's pretend we are home and sing songs." This seemed to help lift their spirits, if only for a few minutes.

Suddenly, the train lost its momentum and came to a halt. A prisoner was lifted on someone's shoulders so he could look out through the small peephole. He couldn't see anything but overheard a conversation between an SS guard and a woman.

"We are from the Red Cross and can give the prisoners some food."

The prisoner came down from the man's shoulders and let the minister try to look out of the peephole. This time, he did have a visual. He saw a sign stating they were in Częstochowa, Poland. He also saw Red Cross trucks with women in white uniforms standing by the train and trying to give them food for the prisoners.

The Nazi guard responded to the Red Cross woman, "These prisoners are thieves. They're going to die anyway, so don't waste your food on them."

The guard took the packages the Red Cross volunteer handed to him and threw them on the ground, stomped on them with his boots, and crushed the contents. With that, the cattle car continued its journey, inching its way toward its unknown destination.

Talking distracted the prisoners from their horrible surroundings, but most of the time they sat in silence and prayed. They shared their limited rations of food.

Two older men died the first day in transit, and their bodies were pushed to the side. A woman removed her shawl and covered the bodies with it. One child saw the corpses and began to cry. A mother nursed her baby, groaned and begged for water. Nobody had any to give her. She collapsed from dehydration. Another person collapsed and then another. It became routine. If the lack of food didn't kill them, the heat and lack of oxygen did. The prisoners kept piling the dead bodies in a corner, and the odors suffused the train. The prisoners traveled under these conditions for a seemingly endless three days and two nights.

Suddenly, the cattle car came to another stop. Everyone held his or her breath in anticipation of what would happen next. Would there be more Red Cross volunteers attempting to give them food, or was it their final destination?

Where are we? What is our new fate?

Once again, the minister climbed up and looked out of the tiny peephole. After a slight pause, he turned to everyone, then quietly and slowly mumbled the painful words:

"I think we'd better all get on our knees and say our final prayers. We will never see Warsaw again."

CHAPTER 9

Expansion of Auschwitz I
—*Arbeit Macht Frei*
[Work Makes You Free]

Mondig was told it was mid-June, 1940, and as the door to the cattle car opened, everyone frantically rushed outside to breathe fresh air. In the haste, some people were pushed to the ground. The prisoners screamed as they tried to get a glimpse of their new surroundings.

What did the minister mean when he said, "We will never see Warsaw again?" Why not? He can't be correct.

As Mondig exited the train, he saw a row of Nazis lined up with machine guns pointing at the prisoners. Guards boarded the cattle car and forced the prisoners to remove the bodies of those unable to walk or those who had died during the transport. Machine guns were aimlessly firing at the new arrivals. Mondig had to step over the dead. He became sick to his stomach but knew he couldn't allow himself to vomit in front of the soldiers standing with their guns. He dared not show weakness. Children clung to their mothers, and wives held onto their husbands tightly. Everyone wanted desperately to survive, although nobody knew what to do.

"Where are we?" people nervously asked each other.

"You are in Auschwitz, and you are here to work," a guard informed them.

Mondig attempted to get a glimpse of his new surroundings and evaluate the *work* that the guard was referring to. He didn't know that he was about to work in the largest Nazi concentration camp, a factory of death, where over one million Jews were to be slaughtered. He was standing on the grounds where the most heinous and despicable acts of cruelty would take place.

Mondig stood in front of army barracks which resembled a broken down military base. He could see there was an enormous amount of work to be done, which would require hard, physical labor.

The early Auschwitz consisted of 22 pre-war barracks—eight two-storey and 14 one-storey barracks.

15 new SS guards arrived approximately at the same time Mondig did. Local residents from the city of Oswiecim also worked in the camp, cleaning the barracks and grounds. Commandant Rudolf Höss had grandiose plans for the prisoners.

Chaos prevailed at the train platform. Unlike the organization at the prisons, it appeared that the soldiers had no cohesive plan and did not work cooperatively. This horrified Mondig. He had never seen anything like this—not even when he was a Polish soldier. There were loud voices yelling at the prisoners and soldiers giving contradictory orders. People were running all over. Bedlam continued until, finally, a commandant succeeded in organizing the events to follow.

A guard ordered two prisoners to collect all the dead bodies and throw them in a pile. All 728 transports had to be accounted for, even those who died during the trip or perhaps escaped.

"Who isn't here?" asked a guard.

What a stupid question. Did the Nazis really expect that someone could have escaped through that infinitesimal hole and be able to answer that he or she wasn't here?

A list of the prisoners was given to an SS guard, and as each person heard his name, he stepped forward and identified himself. The prisoners were instructed to leave their belongings in a pile. Everyone obeyed without questioning the authority. Mondig was surprised but relieved that, as of yet, no one questioned his religion. He hoped to remain viewed as a Polish political prisoner as he embarked into this new, bleak chapter of his life.

Several of the prisoners were placed in quarantine. The guard ordered the other new arrivals to march to their sleeping quarters. The first stop was a delousing shower, which always caused Mondig's heart to skip a beat. He was concerned the others would see he was circumcised and know he was Jewish. However, at this point, the last thing people were concerned about was looking at another prisoner's naked body. After their shower, the prisoners stood in line to get their new uniforms.

There was a pile of assorted shoes. They were told to take one pair each. Mondig asked a friend what size shoes he thought he should get. Mondig was a size 11½ in Poland, but German sizes were different. He took a pair, but they were too big. He returned them. He was yelled at and informed that exchanges were not permitted. They were told to keep their clothes clean, as this was all they would get; a pair of trousers and a shirt to last a lifetime, however long that might be.

And how am I suppose to keep my clothes clean?

Mondig was amazed at the hypocrisy of it all.

The German asked each prisoner if he or she had a trade.

What trade do I have? I was a businessman in Warsaw. Does that count? I entertained the Nazis with heinous acts of cruelty in the prison. Can I say I am an entertainer?

The first logical trade that came to mind was a butcher.

"I am a butcher," Mondig called out, thinking maybe he would be allowed to work in the kitchen and get more food.

"We don't need butchers," the German replied.

"I am also a construction worker," blurted Mondig, thinking they would want people with building experience. The Nazis didn't know he had never used a hammer other than hanging up a picture in his living room.

They were soon marched to a brick building on the other side of the camp, known as Block 11. The barrack was in terrible condition, boards missing from the floor and splinters in the wood. There was no heat, and the cells were small and dark. Mondig was put into a holding cell in the basement with four other prisoners—standing room only.

The guards gave the prisoners postcards and pens and instructed them, "Write to your families. I will tell you what to write. You are to say you are safe and well. Tell them you are working in a shoe factory. Also, write that you are being fed well and taken care of."

Fearful of the consequences if they disobeyed, everyone followed the commands. However, Mondig was swift in his thinking and considered his options. He didn't want to give them his real address, which would enable the Nazis to locate his family. He didn't want them to know where his family was—or at least where he hoped they were. He wrote a fictitious address on the envelope. He nudged Chaim, whom he befriended on the train, and advised him of his trick. He was pleased that he had outsmarted his enemy.

The Nazis can be fooled.

The Germans forced Mondig to return to the standing cell in the basement with his four cellmates, where the cruelty commenced. They were not given any food for two days. Two small holes in the wall provided limited ventilation and a tiny peephole the size of a quarter. Mondig looked out of the hole and saw what seemed to be a groomed courtyard with a high wall in the back. Later he found out that the wall was nicknamed the infamous *Death Wall*, where constant shooting executions took place. The sound of the rifle going off became a dreaded, familiar sound. Every Monday, Thursday, and Saturday, shootings occurred. People were instructed to strip and lean against the Death Wall, only to be shot. Dead bodies covered the earth. Mondig didn't know what was worse, seeing the dead bodies or seeing the apparent pleasure the Nazis had in shooting these innocent people. It was a heartbreaking sight, one Mondig would never be able to erase from his memory.

The prisoners had to stand up straight all night and work during the day. On the third day, they were transferred to a regular cell. They were able to sleep at night in the new cell—albeit on a bare floor. But it was better than standing. In the evenings, if Mondig was lucky, he was given a bowl of bitter soup and a piece of hard, stale bread. He never knew what he was eating, but for the time being, Mondig was grateful he had something to put in his mouth. It was better than nothing. He needed whatever nutrition he could get.

Once again, they were reminded that they were needed to build and glorify Auschwitz I, although at that time, they didn't fully comprehend the extent or purpose of the expansion. Prisoners from Sachsenhausen concentration camp in Germany arrived to assist with the construction. The prisoners were merely informed that the expansion was necessary to accommodate the anticipated large number of newcomers. This was certainly not the shoe factory he was expecting. Each prisoner worked at least 10 hours a day, removing plaster from the old barracks, building the kitchen, lifting heavy sand, digging drainage ditches, moving bricks, or building paths. The previous horse stables were converted into *Blocks*, or barracks.

Mondig became one of the original construction workers of the infamous mass-murder concentration camp of Auschwitz. In the future, he would tremble when he thought of what he had been forced to do.

How does one live with this guilt?

The routine at Auschwitz I became meticulously structured. Daily activities included long *appels* [roll call]. The prisoners lined up at the assembly square and were counted. This occurred several times a day and lasted many hours, with no exceptions. The SS carried out executions at will, on the portable gallows, during roll call.

Mondig wasn't familiar with physical labor of this magnitude. However, he was relatively strong, and his determination gave him the strength to persevere. He still hoped to see his family again, although he didn't know where or when.

After all, wasn't hope what kept the Jewish people alive?

He had to devise a plan to outsmart the perpetrators. He had a few advantages over others: his physical strength, his fluency in several languages, his Aryan appearance, his resilient spirit, and his uncanny ability to be quick with his tongue.

Are people permitted to escape torture at someone else's expense? Why isn't G-d helping us when we need Him?

At that precise moment, Mondig decided he was the only one who could help himself, and he swore to do whatever he could to prevent the Nazis from murdering him.

Mondig often pinched his cheeks to get color in his face so he looked healthy and fit to work. He stood erect when spoken to. However, even with all the survival strategies, he knew what he needed most was *good luck*. So far, he had managed to get by. Only months after Mondig's arrival, the original count of the eight Jewish Polish prisoners had increased to several hundred Jews.

Mondig managed to survive in Block 11—a miracle in itself. Most people didn't survive one week. Nothing could be worse than Block 11. Mondig could not even estimate the number of prisoners he saw shot at the Death Wall and then thrown into mass graves.

By the fall of 1941, the basement of Block 11 was sealed and used for experimentation of Zyklon B, a gas form of hydrocyanic acid that became active on contact with air. It had previously been used as a pesticide to kill lice in prisoners' clothes and proved to be highly effective. The Nazis concluded that if it could kill lice, it could kill humans. Unfortunately, they were correct.

Commandant Karl Fritzsch experimented with the effects of Zyklon B on people. He used 600 Soviet prisoners and 250 patients from the hospital. Within a few minutes, all the "subjects" were dead. By early 1942, Zyklon B became the preferred killing tool of the Nazis. It was packed in small canisters and put into the showerheads. The pellets turned into gas when they were exposed to air. The prisoners were told they were to be given a shower. Instead, they were to inhale the poisonous fumes released from the showerheads and die shortly after. Zyklon B turned out to be the most potent technique for murdering people.

The only challenge the Nazis encountered was how much Zyklon B was needed to kill the greatest number of people in the shortest amount of time. They wanted to be cost effective and maximize the usage of their killing materials.

* * *

Mondig and his fellow inmates were transferred to different barracks. He didn't complain about the transfer, although each transfer left uncertainty. The guards forced the prisoners to walk along a narrow, pebbled path until a sign was visible. For the first time, Mondig saw the German words written above a gate, *Arbeit Macht Frei*. Mondig knew this meant, *Work Makes You Free*. It seemed a bit hypocritical, as Mondig had never worked harder in his life, but he certainly wasn't *free*. In the distance, he saw a church with a cross and pretty buildings. He chuckled at the sight of the church.

Are people really praying there? Are they praying for us? He didn't really think so.

"*Aufmerksamkeit* [Pay attention]," a commandant shouted, calling the people to attention again. "Line up, five across. Who speaks German?" the commandant questioned.

"I do," Mondig quickly responded. Mondig had hoped that his fluency in Polish, German, and English would somehow help him. He knew he would have no need for his Yiddish.

"Good. Tell the people in Polish to stay together."

Mondig translated the German orders. More orders came, and Mondig continued to do as told. The commandant was pleased he had found a prisoner who was fluent in German and Polish and quick to respond to orders. Mondig was the unofficial translator.

Before entering their new barracks, the prisoners were permitted to shower. Each shower made Mondig fear that the truth of his Jewishness would be uncovered. During the cattle train ride to Auschwitz, the eight Jewish prisoners had agreed they would help each other and try to conceal their identity as Jews. Each shower was the test.

How long can we trick the enemy? Will our luck run out? Will our pact be sincere?

Mondig trusted no one anymore.

The prisoners began to undress. Mondig and his friend Jacob stayed close to each other in an attempt to conceal their Jewish identity—their circumcisions. However, a Yugoslavian prisoner bumped into them, and when Mondig reacted impulsively lifting his hands in the air, the Yugoslavian saw Mondig's *secret.* He saw Jacob's as well. As had been discovered in the prison, Mondig's circumcision revealed his true identity – Jewish.

There was a scream. "*Juden hier* [There are Jews here]."

A guard blew his piercing whistle, and more guards entered. They beat both Mondig and Jacob. A grinning German took a chair and broke it into pieces as he hit Mondig on the head. Another guard brutally hit Jacob across the face with his club. Blood poured down his cheeks. Jacob's eye began to swell. A Nazi jumped from behind and lashed out at Mondig and then Jacob with his long, sharp whip. The other prisoners watched in horror. At the end of the melee, Mondig's body was black and blue, swollen, and bled profusely. He felt as if his limbs had been torn out of his body. Jacob, also badly beaten, just sank to the earth.

An SS guard instructed Mondig to drag Jacob outside. "He won't be able to work, so he is of no use to us."

Mondig himself could barely move but mustered the strength to drag Jacob outside the shower house. Jacob's wails added to the disturbing background noise.

"Please leave him alone. He has suffered enough." Mondig begged.

Ignoring Mondig, the guard shot Jacob in the chest. Mondig's body froze, thinking his turn would be next, but he was spared.

He closed his eyes, recited the familiar mourner's *Kaddish*, and concluded by saying, "*Shema Yisrael, Adonai Eloheinu, Adonai Ehad.*"

Mondig sadly looked at his friend for the last time. Now the group of eight Jews from Tarnow was reduced to seven.

CHAPTER 10
A New Name
—Number 31321

"All prisoners report to the yard," ordered *Hauptmann* [Captain] Gustav.

The hauptmann walked up and down the lines, viewing the prisoners. "Those who feel too sick to work today, step forward," he commanded. Hoping for a day's rest from work, several men stepped forward.

Unknowingly, they had sealed their fate. Hauptmann Gustav turned to the other officers and said, "Take them away."

The prisoners were led away, never seen or heard from again. Hauptmann Gustav approached Mondig and stopped. He stared at him, smirked, and commented, "Why do you look so good? Aren't you working hard enough?" And he whipped him.

Mondig didn't budge. He was used to the whipping by now, as flogging was common in Block 11. The hauptmann turned to the remaining Jews and continued in a softer, calmer voice. "You will see I am really a kind man. I am not like the other Nazis. I will allow you to take a shower once a week. I'll see that you are well fed and well clothed. There's a lot of work to be done here. We're expecting more prisoners every day, and we need to build more barracks for them. I have strict guidelines and deadlines to meet. If you work well for me and make me look good, I will help you."

The prisoners wanted to believe him and hoped he would be true to his word. He was the first German officer who offered any indication of sympathetic words or encouragement.

* * *

Hauptmann Gustav was ordered to send 50 Jews to start the construction of additional barracks. Mondig was one of the prisoners selected. His assignment was to dig ditches and split rails. By March 1, 1941, *Reichsführer-SS* Heinrich Himmler issued an order to enlarge the camp to accommodate 30,000 prisoners.

Barracks were built for different purposes—Block 24 infirmary; Block 7 aristocrats; Block 47 the *Reichsdeuctsche* [Aryan criminals]; Block 49 *kapos'* quarters; Block 30 offices; Block 29 camp brothel.

Mondig had difficulty falling asleep that night and wondered what the future had in store for them.

A new hauptmann, a new work assignment? What does that mean?

Again, he tossed and turned, thinking about his fate.

Gustav's words kept resonating in his mind: "Get some sleep. We need to build more barracks. We need to build more barracks." That was not a good sign

Why are they continuously expanding the camp? What are the Nazis going to do with all these people?

It had already grown tremendously since Mondig first arrived.

Nobody ever saw Hauptmann Gustav again. There was never any mention of his disappearance. Mondig wondered if he was transferred or got punished for being too lenient with the prisoners.

That evening, Mondig saw a friend of his bent over in the barracks with a look of pain and fear written all over his face. Mondig approached him and asked what happened. Without speaking, his friend lifted the leg of his uniform and showed Mondig his badly beaten, broken leg with the bones protruding from the skin. Mondig was horrified when his friend told him the guard attacked him solely because he asked permission to urinate.

"Anything can happen here. There are no limits as to what the Nazis are capable of doing," his friend cried to him.

"I know, but we must be brave," Mondig tried to reassure him.

"All is lost. Look at me. My leg is broken. I can't walk. My belly is swollen. I am starving. I can't survive. This place is unlivable." His friend lost hope.

"My friend. You are wrong. We need to hold onto our faith and strength. Think of what the Jews have endured throughout history. Did we give up when we were slaves in Egypt? Of course not. Didn't the Jews wander through the Sinai desert for 40 years? Didn't we overcome many obstacles? And with all the hardships encountered, didn't Jews live to cross over the Red Sea into Canaan, the Promised Land? And, my friend, hold on to your life. We will also conquer!" Mondig consoled him.

In October 1941, Mondig was sent to a barrack in Auschwitz II–Birkenau which was an old stall, used by the Polish army to house horses. The tethering rings were still in place. He estimated that it once had accommodated 50 horses. However, approximately 100 prisoners were forced to live in the crowded, unsanitary quarters. The stalls contained three levels of wooden bunks, each level divided into cubbies lined with a thin straw mattress. Several inmates shared a cubby. One always hoped for good, trusting "bed companions" as they slept touching each other, breathing on each other and exchanging sweat under the same blanket. The lucky ones got to sleep on the highest level, as the wood frequently collapsed, landing on those on the bottom level. They slept fully dressed, with the one uniform allotted them. Insects and vermin also shared the straw mattresses with the inmates. The barracks lacked heat, electricity, and running water. Rats and lice plagued the prisoners. Additionally, there were no plumbing facilities, and due to prisoners' dysentery, the foul odor of feces permeated the building.

Auschwitz II–Birkenau was in the village of Brzezinka (Birkenau), several kilometers away from the main camp of Auschwitz, although most transports didn't arrive in Birkenau until 1942. The residents living in the surrounding areas were evicted from their homes. Birkenau was to be a secure camp with a buffer zone around it, isolated from the Polish population. It was initially intended for 200,000 prisoners of war. From its inception, it became an integral part of the Auschwitz concentration camp and was instrumental in the mass extermination of the Jews.

The first undertakings at Birkenau included dismantling the current buildings, gathering materials needed, leveling the marsh terrain, and building a road adjacent to the railroad tracks that would bring the prisoners to their final destination.

Mondig noticed the increase in the number of attack

dogs. The man-eating dogs were referred to as *mensch* [Yiddish for "good person"], and the Jews were referred to as *dogs*. He sensed this camp would be more horrific than Auschwitz I, and he was correct. Ultimately, he found out the fate of Birkenau—a death camp, with one purpose: to rapidly annihilate the Jewish race. The only way to describe the future Birkenau was *Hell on Earth*. There would be no place in the world that could compare to Birkenau. It was to be the greatest example of man's inhumanity to human beings in history.

The *Final Solution*, the elimination of all the Jews, was decided upon on January 20, 1942 at the Wannsee Conference in Berlin. The Nazis concluded that based on their experiments, gassing the Jews in the extermination camps would be the most effective means to expeditiously exterminate the entire race.

Five crematoriums (two large crematoria and two smaller ones) were expected to be completed including three adjacent areas with an undressing room and a large gas chamber. The crematorium ovens would dispose of 4,500 corpses a day. The ashes were to be used as fertilizer as no part of the human remains were to be wasted.

Sonderkommandos [units of Jewish prisoners often referred to as "bearers of secrets"], had no choice but to follow orders, which included checking the mouths of dead bodies for gold fillings and moving corpses from the gas chamber to the crematoriums. The *Sonderkommandos* commonly came in full view of corpses of family members or friends. Although Mondig's work assignment was physically strenuous, having to push enormous boulders that were obstructing the path, he was relieved that he wasn't forced to do the job of a *Sonderkommando*. Moving heavy boulders required a considerable amount of strength, which he barely had anymore, but in his mind, disposing of human bodies was even worse. At least there was no human connection with boulders.

Mondig found each day more challenging than the previous one. Almost everyone around him was severely diseased and malnourished. Demands on the prisoners increased. Prisoners who couldn't adhere to the orders were shot. Mondig commonly saw dead, emaciated bodies lying on the damp dirt. The prisoners were not allowed to take a break—not for water and certainly not for the bathroom.

Mondig played mind games to keep his body moving.

Only one more boulder, he would reassure himself.

To the others, he would say, "One more day. The end will come." He never allowed the thought of giving up to cross his mind. He would count backward from one hundred—anything to distract himself. He would try to gain strength from his memories, reflecting on the good times he shared with his family.

But then the recurring guilt set in.

Why did I take the path of least resistance and do nothing? Why did I close my eyes to what was happening in front of me, and how did I possibly think of Hitler as only a fly in a bucket? Why didn't I take my family and leave Poland when I could? I was so stupid for not listening to the warnings and closing my eyes to the truth. It is my own fault that I am living in Hell, and I don't even know if my family is living at all. I am responsible for my family's fate.

Mondig cursed and blamed himself for his situation and for not saving his family. He thought he could have and should have done something.

Mondig was constantly hungry. The meager rations were barely enough to give him the strength needed to move boulders. He licked the bottom of his bowl to make sure he didn't leave anything behind. The bread tasted like sawdust. The meat and vegetables were rotten and were unsuitable for a dog. Dehydration, hunger, and disease were prevalent among the prisoners. Each day was a struggle, and a day didn't pass without a comrade he knew dying.

Death had become routine.

Who was murdered today?

Mondig sometimes was lucky and found things on the ground. He never passed anything by. Everything had a purpose. He took scraps of paper to be used as toilet paper. He also took left-over wire which he used to mend buttons on his jacket with. Nothing was wasted.

* * *

By 1943 and 1944, prisoners were arriving in droves from virtually every German-occupied country of Europe—France, Belgium, Holland, Slovakia, Croatia, and Norway.

November 29, 1943 was another date Mondig would never forget. He moved to new sleeping quarters—a different barrack in Birkenau. The commandant Rudolf Höss instructed the SS guards to round up the prisoners and march them to a building. The prisoners were told they would get a number stamped on their left forearms that would replace their names. Auschwitz was the only camp to tattoo numbers on prisoners' arms, which were used for identification purposes.

Hans, the German in charge of Mondig's group, instructed the prisoners to form a straight line in alphabetical order. When it was Mondig's turn to approach the table, he rolled up his left sleeve as ordered and within seconds had the number 31321 tattooed on his arm, never to be erased. The prisoners were reminded that whenever they were addressed or spoken to, they would respond with their numbers and not their names. They were stripped of their names and their identities, adding to the Nazis' already long list of dehumanization efforts. The Nazi process was complete. They had successfully depleted Mondig of his entire life—his family, his livelihood, his home, his country, his clothes, and finally, his name. After already having had several names—Moishe, Moniek, and Mondig—he was now *officially* registered in Birkenau and reduced to a number… 31321.

CHAPTER 11

Can Anyone Survive Hell in Auschwitz II–Birkenau?

The Nazis had visions of Birkenau consisting of over 300 brick and wood buildings, divided among several fields. As in Auschwitz I, inmates were plagued by lack of water, terrible sanitary conditions and barbaric abuse. Many barracks were built without a foundation, lying directly on the swampy, compressed earth. There was a long bench in the middle of each barrack with holes cut out on the top. They were used as latrines. The prisoners were given several minutes each morning and evening to publicly squat and relieve themselves. Vomit and human feces that missed the hole surrounded the latrine. Needless to say, the smell was suffocating. It was bitterly cold in the winter and extremely hot in the summer. The prisoners had one goal—stay alive.

The routine in Birkenau was similar to Auschwitz I. The day started early at 4:30 a.m. with reveille and roll call. Upon awaking, Mondig and his bed companions quickly arranged their shared thin blanket on the straw mattress. Mondig checked to see that his fingernails were short, as required. He cut them by using his teeth as no scissors were provided. During roll call the prisoners stood at attention in rows of five, unless directed otherwise. This sometimes took hours. As your number was called, you responded. Everyone's number was permanently engraved in his memory. Nobody had to look at his arm to be reminded of it. Daily instructions were given and drudgeries were assigned to each prisoner. Dead bodies had to be accounted for.

After the roll call Mondig and the other prisoners lined up for "food", clutching their one bowl and spoon. The workday was typically from 6:00 a.m. to 12:00 noon and resumed at 12:30 p.m. until 7:00 p.m. Prisoners were escorted to their work assignment under strict supervision. In the evening, they returned for another roll call. Lights usually went off at 9 p.m., although many prisoners had difficulty falling asleep. Mondig was one of them. Although he was always tired, his fatigue was camouflaged by his state of constant anxiety.

As Mondig was absorbed in thought, Shlomo, a *kapo* [a Jew who was assigned by the SS guards to supervise forced labor] entered and ordered the prisoners to line up outside. This particular morning, the *kapo* asked, "Who is a blacksmith? Who is a tailor?"

As each profession was called, prisoners stepped forward, and they were directed to different lines. Mondig was worried. He had once told the officers he was a butcher, but that didn't work to his advantage. He also said he was a construction worker, which did help. But what profession did they need now?

"Who is a carpenter?" the prisoners were asked. Mondig thought he could qualify for this job.

How is a carpenter different from a construction worker? I've already built many paths and buildings in Auschwitz I. In fact, I was one of the men who built Block 18.

"I am a carpenter and can build barracks for all the prisoners you want. I have already built roads and moved heavy boulders. I am very strong and determined. I can do whatever you want." Mondig hoped he had a third of the strength he claimed he had, as his strength was deteriorating.

The *kapo* grinned, as he knew Mondig was a good worker. He pointed to the work line for Mondig to join.

Years earlier, Mondig questioned how one Jew could go against another Jew. He remembered his son also had a strong opinion about this. Mondig still pondered this moral conflict.

How can a Jew build facilities that would ultimately lead to the destruction of his own people?

By now, Mondig was fully aware of the purpose of the camp.

Will I be considered an accomplice to the Nazi crimes? Will people call me a traitor? What about the Jews who actually march the victims into the gas chamber to face their death or those who move their dead corpses into the ovens? Is that worse than what I do? What is the criteria for judging right and wrong? Who has the right to judge if he or she is not in that life-or-death situation?

Should a Jew be held accountable for complying with Nazis' orders with the purpose of preserving himself? To what degree is Jewish cooperation with the Nazis acceptable?

This moral conflict lay deep in Mondig's heart, and although he did not have an immediate answer, he understood the primacy of survival. For him, he felt building and constructing Auschwitz was terrible, but he reasoned that if he didn't do it, someone else would. Each prisoner had to decide his own limitations and what his conscience would allow him to do as a matter of survival a way to stand up to the Nazis. Hopefully, Mondig, by complying with the Nazi orders for the time being, would find a way to escape and alert others. He longed to spread the news to the world about the atrocities that he'd seen.

His train of thought was broken when Mondig heard a frail man scream, "Shoot me. I can't live like this." His plea was ignored.

He was told by the Nazi, "I won't waste a bullet on you. You are so sick-looking, you will die without a bullet."

Will it ever end?

Mondig told himself again he would do everything in his power not to die at the hands of a Nazi. He was going to decide when and where he would die, even if that meant taking his own life.

Shlomo explained to the prisoners the plans for the third expansion of Birkenau, which Mondig had already heard more times than he wanted to remember. Shlomo pointed to the areas where buildings needed to be erected, and he warned them of the consequences if they tried to escape.

"Look at the fence that separates you from the women. You see the barbed wire? It is electrified. Behind it is deep water. If you touch it, you will die a painful death." He paused and then continued, "Notice the four corners of the camp. There are watch towers at each corner guarded with SS guards ready to shoot you anytime. They observe every move you make. There are man-killing German shepherd dogs all over, and they will eat you alive if you try anything stupid. For your sake, don't even think about it."

He refrained from pointing out a building—a crematorium. The façade of the building was deceiving as it was decorative on the outside and had gardens and trees surrounding it. It was situated in the back of the camp, out of view from the train station and the new arrivals. The infamous slogan among the guards was, "The only way out of here is through the chimney."

When Mondig considered planning his escape, his mind drifted to an earlier attempt by another prisoner in the fall of 1940, and the consequences everyone suffered. All the inmates were required to stand at attention for 24 hours as the Nazis searched for the escapee. It was extremely hot, and Mondig perspired profusely. Nobody was allowed to move or speak. Mondig believed he would not survive. With the slightest movement, the SS guard would approach you and whip you. When the captive was finally found, he was forced to march around the other prisoners screaming, "I returned. I am slime."

The Nazi soldier shouted to the prisoners, "I will show you what happens if you try to escape," and he proceeded to torture the captive. In full view, his arm was severed and he was stabbed in various parts of his body to set an example to the others. The prisoners were not allowed to return to the barracks until the man was declared dead, 14 hours later.

That night the prisoners were extremely quiet. Earlier, Mondig had been able to steal an extra portion of bread. He took it from his straw mattress, where he had hidden it, and offered bites to others. "We must not give up." With that, they sang a few songs, and a few of them fell asleep.

The transports escalated, and more prisoners continued to arrive daily from all across Europe— Soviet prisoners of war, Gypsies, Czechs, Yugoslavs, French, Austrians, and Germans; primarily Jewish. 500 political prisoners arrived from Warsaw on one cattle car alone. The numbers were staggering.

Commandant Höss again reiterated to the prisoners, "We still need more barracks for all these prisoners. You must work harder and build them faster."

Nazi Herr Miller implemented Commandant Höss's orders. "Follow me," Miller shouted as he led the prisoners to the area where ditches were to be dug and more barracks were to be built. Mondig's work assignment was harder than ever. He was forced to split rails, dig ditches, and push a rolling machine with other prisoners for hours at a time. If he stopped to rest, he was beaten with a whip or a club. Several prisoners were harnessed to a plow as if they were horses. Some of the prisoners couldn't endure the brutality and deliberately threw themselves against the electric fence that surrounded the camp and died instantly.

By the end of 1943, one of the new arrivals told Mondig about the events that transpired in his hometown—the Warsaw ghetto uprising. He was informed that thousands of Jews lived underground illegally and tried to hide from their German enemy. Mordecai Anielewicz was the brave commander of the Jewish Combat Organization and planned the uprising.

On January 18, 1943, the German troops surrounded the ghetto, but the Jews fought back and held their ground. On April 19, 1943, 2,000 SS troops entered the ghetto armed with tanks. They were shocked by the Jewish resistance and were forced to withdraw from the ghetto. Mondig felt national pride for his country and proud of his fellow Warsaw Jews for their courage and heroic acts. However, the Jewish underground was no match for Germany's heavy artillery. The Warsaw ghetto soon became a cemetery and ceased to exist.

The Jewish community of Warsaw almost completely vanished from the face of the earth along with its synagogues and Jewish schools. The thought that the place he grew up in no longer existed was earth-shattering.

Have I been stripped of my entire childhood?

Even if Mondig miraculously survived, where would he go? His city was destroyed.

By chance, Mondig happened to cross paths with Itzhak, one of the Jews who had been first incarcerated in the Polish prison with him. "What work do you do?" asked Mondig. "You don't look as if you are starving."

Itzhak was silent.

"What is your secret? We've been through so much together. You can tell me anything," Mondig reassured his friend.

"I work in the gas chambers," Itzhak confessed. "I remove the bodies after they have been gassed and take them to the crematorium. I don't like doing this, but I get extra privileges. I am in a *Sonderkommando*."

Mondig was shocked. He never stood in front of a Jew who served in a *Sonderkommando*. It gave him the chills. Although he couldn't fathom the idea of seeing Jewish corpses and disposing of them, Itzhak's words of extra *privileges* resonated with him.

What did that mean? Privileges?

Months dragged on. One afternoon, an announcement blasted throughout the camp. "All men report to the yard." Everyone knew that an unexpected roll call most often meant another attempted escape. Mondig rushed to the roll call as he knew the consequences of tardiness.

A heavy-set, stone-faced Nazi stationed himself in front of the prisoners and grunted, "We warned you not to try to escape." He paused and then continued, "Number 65423 was caught trying to cut the barbed wire. Take a good look at him."

The Nazi pointed to a Jew with his hands tied behind his back, slumped over in front of the inmates. "You will all watch as this man is hanged. It will teach you a lesson not to try to escape."

The Nazi blew his whistle and his two assistants

grabbed the prisoner, dragged him to the scaffold, placed a noose around his neck, and hung him.

Mondig felt a sharp tightening in the pit of his stomach. After the hanging, the Nazis continued to call each person's number. The Nazis seemed thrilled to extend the torture by forcing the prisoners to remain standing at attention until all the numbers were called. It was now winter, and the prisoners, clad only in their light, striped gray-and-white prison uniforms, nearly froze. Not far from Mondig an older man collapsed to the ground, never to get up.

"Return to work," the Nazi ordered. It was a typical day in the camp.

* * *

"My name is Max, and I'm now in charge here," Max said, introducing himself.

Max, a *kapo*, was probably in his late thirties. He, like Mondig, had typical Aryan features—blond hair and blue eyes—and he weighed about 180 pounds. He was very strict with the 100 Jews he was in charge of, as he wanted to convince the Germans of his value to them. He wanted his prisoners to obey him, thus making his job easier. He liked having two cups of coffee in the morning, and he appointed Mondig as his daily coffee supplier.

Mondig thought to himself, *I'm taking a risk getting a second cup of coffee. Everyone knows we are only permitted one cup a day. However, if I refuse, he will certainly shoot me, even though he is a fellow Jew. If I get caught by the SS, they will surely shoot me. Either way, I will be dead. But, if I can get Max a second cup of coffee, maybe he will help me.*

And so for the next few weeks, Mondig took his chances. When an officer brought the coffee pot to the courtyard, Mondig stood in line with the others. He drank his cup of coffee and then snuck onto another line to get a second cup for Max, hoping he wouldn't be recognized. Max was grateful for the coffee and gave Mondig extra portions of food whenever possible. One morning, however, while Mondig was serving Max his coffee, Mondig tripped and accidentally spilled the coffee on Max's uniform. Mondig was petrified and quickly apologized. There was nothing more Mondig could do or say, and he just hoped that Max would understand and forget the incident. Later in the afternoon, while bending over, splitting a rail, Mondig felt a jolt on his back. Before he had time to stand up, he received another hard blow. And another. Someone was hitting him with a heavy rail. Mondig finally turned around and saw Max still holding the rail in his right hand. He was ready to hit Mondig again, which probably would have killed him.

Mondig jumped up and exclaimed, "Max, please. Wait! I have a gold watch, which I hid when I arrived here. It is worth a lot of money. I'll give it to you if you don't hit me again."

Max's eyes opened wide, and he accepted the offer. "Meet me in the barracks later," he said as he dropped the rail to the ground, sparing Mondig.

Mondig's life may have been spared for the moment, but his fears elevated. He had lied to Max. He did not have a gold watch anymore. His watch had been confiscated at the prison. He knew he dared not meet Max, as agreed. That would be his death sentence. He didn't even know where he could hide or what to do. The injuries he sustained from the beating were intense, and he was certain he had several broken bones. He was sapped of all his strength. Slowly dragging his body on all fours, he managed to sneak into the closest barracks and collapsed.

When he woke up from his unconscious state, he found himself in the prisoner-operated *krankenbau* [infirmary]. He had no recollection of how he got there. It was strange to Mondig that there was an infirmary in the killing center. On one hand, they were killing people, but on the other hand, they were healing people. It just didn't make sense. The infirmary was crowded, and it took a long time before the doctor, a rather small man in a dirty white cloak, approached him and asked him where he was from. They spoke softly, and the doctor revealed that he was a Jewish doctor in his hometown, Krakow, Poland.

What a stroke of good luck meeting a Jewish doctor from Krakow.

Mondig shared his background with him, and, surprisingly, the doctor and Mondig had a personal connection. The doctor was familiar with Mondig's clothing store in Warsaw and had shopped there whenever he visited his family. He remembered Mondig's father, and how nice he was. The doctor asked how Mondig sustained the injuries, but Mondig was terrified to tell him that Kapo Max had brutally hit him. He didn't know if Max and the doctor were friends.

Mondig merely shrugged his shoulders. He begged the doctor to transfer him into another barrack and give him a less strenuous job. He needed to hide from Max. Mondig was petrified that if Max found him, he would demand the gold watch, which he didn't have, and then kill him. He also needed a break from the brutal work.

The doctor disappeared for a short time and returned with good news. "A friend of mine owes me a favor. He is willing to help you. You will be transferred to Block 26. You will work in the Canada warehouse, where you will be treated better and receive extra *privileges*." Mondig remembered hearing those words before—extra privileges. He liked the news.

Mondig also remembered one of the inmates telling him about the Canada warehouse, a storehouse overflowing with possessions confiscated from the prisoners. It was thought to have been nicknamed "Canada" after the country Canada to symbolize the wealth Canada represented. Mondig hoped that his new assignment would be easier than what he had been subjected to before.

Mondig stayed in the infirmary two days. The doctor visited him both days. During one visit, the doctor friend described the infirmary. It had a surgical department and operating room. Dr. Mengele was the chief physician who specialized in conducting experimental medical tests on captive twins. Dr. Mengele injected serum into the eyeballs of dozens of children to determine if he could change the color of their eyes. Another experiment included injecting chloroform into the hearts of twins to observe if they both would die at the same time. He also focused on sterilization and fertility experiments, in an effort to find methods to increase the German birth rate. Jews were sterilized by being subjected to high doses of radiation, which burnt the reproductive organs of men and women. The doctor then removed parts of the women's reproductive organs and castrated the men. The experiments were conducted without any regard for safety of the human subjects, and without any anesthesia.

Mondig was almost sorry he had even heard this. He didn't want to know more details. It made him sick to his stomach.

Slowly, Mondig's injuries healed. He was discharged and sent to the new barrack, and commenced work in the Canada warehouse.

The work in the Canada warehouse proved to be significantly easier than the physical labor assignments. The warehouse was located a few hundred yards from the gas chamber, which Mondig deliberately avoided looking at. Mondig's new assignment was to go to the *Judenrampe* [selection ramp] when the transports arrived, collect the luggage and belongings from the newly arrived prisoners, and take everything to the Canada warehouse. He then sorted the belongings, which were ultimately transported to Germany for use by the Nazis. Sorting the items entailed opening the suitcases, displaying all the possessions on a table in full view, and organizing them in appropriate piles: cognac, tapestries, cigarettes, money, clothes.

The SS men oversaw the Canada warehouse but were lax in doing so. They, too, benefited from the property of the murdered victims and indulged themselves by "borrowing" things. In fact, many of the belongings were illegally sold in the largest black market in Europe at the time. Mondig quickly surmised that if he was clever and swift, his assignment would give him an opportunity to "borrow" valuables that he could later use for barter or bribery. He was going to do his best to get the extra privileges he had heard prisoners refer to.

Trains constantly left for Germany packed with confiscated Jewish goods, but there were so many items that the storehouses always remained full to capacity, leaving a great quantity behind. There weren't enough trains to transport all the possessions.

The prisoners were treated better at the Canada warehouse, which buoyed Mondig's spirits. Some women prisoners were even allowed to let their hair grow. Working in this warehouse was better than splitting rails or building barracks in the hot sun or frigid winter. Occasionally, Mondig even got an extra portion of food, sometimes enough for him to smuggle to his hungry friends.

One afternoon, while opening a suitcase, he spoke with a German prisoner, Bruno Chernafsky. Bruno had been given a life sentence for an alleged bank robbery. He currently served as an *Oberkapo* [supervisor of prisoners]. Mondig suspected he had influence on the SS guards. By chance, one day Mondig came across two packages of chocolate lying on the ground. He quickly grabbed them and hid them in his uniform trousers. Later, he gave an appreciative Bruno the chocolate. Mondig learned an easy, although risky, way to appease the superiors. Kapo Max had liked coffee; Bruno liked chocolate.

Unlike most of the prisoners, Mondig befriended a Nazi guard, Herr Schilinger. He was an enormous man and feared by many inmates. For no apparent reason, every morning after breakfast, he would circle the area, take out his gun, and start shooting randomly, screaming, "*Ich bin Berliner* [I am from Berlin]." Nobody cared where he was from.

Mondig placated him and gave him *extras* he was able to sneak out of the Canada warehouse, always trying to stay on his good side. He wasn't going to let

Schilinger think he was intimidated, but he wasn't going to be defiant. Not yet.

By now, the trains carrying the Jews arrived at an even faster pace, sometimes several transports in a given day. There were more guards on the selection platform with additional dogs nearby, ready to attack at a moment's notice.

Mondig came in contact with the *Angel of Death*, Dr. Josef Mengele, and his assistant, Dr. Blanco, at the selection ramp. He witnessed as Dr. Mengele glanced at the prisoners and, based on his quick visual assessment, sorted the prisoners into three lines—one for the healthy and strong who would work as slave laborers; one for the young, frail, or crippled, who were doomed to die; and the third (mainly twins) for those whom Dr. Mengele or Dr. Blanco deemed candidates for the cruel, deadly human experiments. Dr. Mengele informed the prisoners of their fate by the mere gesture of his finger, indicating which of the three lines the prisoner must go on. Decisions for *those fit to work* were based solely on the person's general appearance and not by any physical examination.

The selection went quickly. The arrival at the selection ramp seemed unusually organized, unlike in the earlier days. There was tight supervision of the transports, preventing prisoners from escaping. Several prisoners were selected to reenter the trains, clean them, and dispose of the human excrement and any belongings left behind. Guards led those on the death line to the undressing room, and commanded them to remove their clothes. They were tricked and told they would get their clothes back after the shower.

Then they were guided into a large shower room, the door was tightly closed, and the gas poured through the vents. A guard witnessed the entire procedure by looking through a peephole. Their fate was sealed, and in a short time there was dead silence. The door was opened. The dead bodies were removed by the *Sonderkommando*. Approximately three bodies were put into one oven at a time. The entire process took 20 minutes.

Those who were classified as fit to work also had their belongings confiscated. They were sent to special rooms to be shaved and disinfected. They then were instructed to shower, men and women together, as the SS sneered at them. Afterward, they were allotted their camp clothing: a gray-and-white-striped camp uniform and wooden clogs. The registration process then took place. The prisoners completed a printed personal-data form—*Häftlings-Personal-Karte*—stating their place of residence, education, occupation, and addresses of relatives. For the final step, the guards took a long needle and tattooed a serial number on the prisoners' left forearm. Auschwitz had such a high rate of mortality that identifying a large number of corpses without a tattoo system would have been difficult. Different series of numbers were introduced at the camp at various times to distinguish groups of prisoners.

Mondig painfully watched the entire selection process, observing innocent people, including women, children, and babies, being given their death sentence. So many times, he wanted to warn the people and scream, "Run!" But he couldn't. Alerting the prisoners of their impending destiny was not in his interest and would have been futile. Mondig knew that if he had any contact with the new arrivals, he would be killed as well.

Although sick to his stomach, he kept his mouth shut and continued to persevere.

One afternoon, when Mondig was working at the Canada warehouse, he noticed a door to a room was slightly ajar. Curious, he peeked in. What he saw terrified him. Piles of skeletal bodies, gold fillings from their teeth, strands of hair, and hundreds of pairs of eyeglasses were scattered around the room. That was the last time he acted on curiosity.

Mondig quickly shut the door and vomited. He had never seen anything so horrific. As sick as he felt, he knew he had to get back to work or they would realize he was missing. He had no time to indulge in self-pity. He composed himself, wiped the vomit off his face, and went back to sorting clothes in the Canada warehouse.

One of the workers noticed his pale appearance and called out, "Mondig. What happened? You look sick. You look as if you have seen a ghost."

Mondig ignored him and looked the other way. He really had seen a ghost.

A Jewish friend of Mondig's had been working in the lumberyard and confiscated several tools. He confided in Mondig and four other friends and shared his plan for an escape. At first Mondig laughed, looking around and seeing the myriad soldiers holding guns at the electrified barbed wire, and of course, the savage-looking dogs. "It's too risky," he commented. "We've survived this long. Let's not ruin it now. We don't have a chance against them. Somebody will come to our rescue. The Americans or the British will surely rescue us."

Where is everyone? Why isn't someone helping us? Is the rest of the word asleep?

His friend told him about Kazimierz Piechowski, a Pole who came to Auschwitz on the second transport from Tarnow. He made a daring escape. "If he can escape, so can we." He persevered and convinced Mondig and the others to join him in planning an escape. He showed them the shovels he had confiscated. The plan was simple. "Every night after the guards check the barracks, we will take turns digging an underground tunnel. I located the ideal spot where the soil is soft. It will be easy. We will take shifts guarding. If you see anyone coming, you will hum *Deutschland Über Alles*."

Although Mondig was skeptical, he decided they had nothing to lose. They would probably die anyway, and better to die resisting than to go up in smoke in a gas chamber. He had made a promise to himself that he would die on his own terms.

In the middle of the night, while others tried to sleep, the prisoners began to execute their plan. Everything seemed to be going well, and after a few months, the tunnel reached the outside fence. They covered the top of the tunnel with grass and twigs. Finally, they thought they were ready to implement part two: the escape. It was now or never. Though petrified, they proceeded. They were divided into teams. The first team of two people squeezed through the hole on their stomachs as the others stood guard. Everything seemed to go smoothly. It was quiet, so Mondig assumed they had reached the outside. Mondig and Stefan were next in line. Jerzey was standing guard. Mondig started to crawl through the tunnel with Stefan close behind him. Mondig looked back but didn't see Jerzey. They needed someone to look out for them, as they did for the first two men. However, the plan didn't consider the possibility of one of them getting panic-stricken. Jerzey panicked and could not continue. He left his post, and a Nazi saw the attempted escape. By now, it was too late for Mondig and Stefan to turn back.

As they emerged on the other side of the tunnel, they were greeted by a German guard screaming, "*Aufhoren* [Halt]. *Achtung* [Danger]."

Mondig froze. The guard seemed intoxicated; he was wobbling and stuttering.

Mondig didn't know what to do.

Bribe the guard?

Somehow, he didn't think that bribery would work this time, although he tried. "I have gold. Don't shoot."

The Nazi officer apparently was too intoxicated to fully understand and started shooting aimlessly. Mondig and Stefan ran, zigging and zagging, dodging the random bullets. They ran as quickly as they could until they spotted a stack of lumber piled high. Mondig pushed some of the lumber aside, and they both slid into the pile. By now, sirens were blasting. The loudspeaker roared, "31321 *Jude* has escaped." SS guards ran all over and dogs howled. One of the Yugoslavian SS guards spotted the suspicious lump in the lumberyard. He moved the lumber and saw Mondig and Stefan. Mondig pushed his hand through the pile of lumber, and as some of the pieces slid away, Mondig yanked the gun from the officer's hand and hit him in the face with it. The officer fell. Mondig and Stefan jumped out of the pile of lumber, and Mondig grabbed the SS guard by the head and bit his neck. Stefan reached for the Nazi's hands and held them tightly behind his back. Mondig and Stefan fought furiously with their attacker. While Stefan held his arms, Mondig delivered a hard kick with all his power into the guard's stomach.

Two other guards joined the brawl. One hit Mondig in the face, and the other hit Stefan on the head. Mondig's nose broke, and four front teeth fell out. The guard took out a knife and stabbed Mondig deep in the back of his neck. He was covered with blood. Stefan also was brutalized. Mondig thought for sure his luck had run out, and he pleaded with them just to shoot him and get it over with. That was the first and only time Mondig went back on his promise to himself and was ready to succumb to his death at the hands of a Nazi. The guard said shooting would be too easy for them. They had to suffer. Mondig and Stefan were sent to solitary confinement as the guards laughed.

* * *

Stefan could barely walk. The guard told him if he couldn't walk into the cell by himself, he would be shot. Stefan tried his best to follow orders, but his badly damaged body couldn't comply. He collapsed. The guard kept his word and shot him in the face—two feet from Mondig. Mondig spent two days in solitary confinement with no food, no light, and no contact with anyone, mourning the loss of yet another friend.

Mondig was told he would remain in solitary confinement for as long as he would live. However, after two days, a guard opened the door and told him, "You've been in the camp so long, we'll see how much longer you can survive on your own." Shockingly, the guard gave him a wet rag to clean himself, a different uniform, and released him. This was truly a miracle.

Maybe there are advantages to being a veteran and having survived so long.

Mondig struggled from his weakened being, but luckily, he wasn't required to do physical labor. Working in the Canada warehouse certainly had its benefits. The other prisoners in the barracks always treated Mondig with respect and helped him, as they admired that he had survived so long and was the veteran among the prisoners. In turn, Mondig gave them extra food that he was given in the Canada warehouse.

A few days later, a captain called on five workers from the Canada, including Mondig, and ordered them to follow him. As usual, Mondig followed, not knowing what to expect. The captain led the men to the familiar selection platform. However, this time an unusually large number of prisoners got off the train. As was customary for Mondig, he always glanced at the people to see if by some slim chance his wife and children were among them. He had mixed feelings. Although he wanted desperately to see them, he didn't want them to suffer this nightmare. That day, he spotted Rachel, a wealthy woman who had owned a jewelry shop in

Warsaw not far from his business. Mondig made it a rule never to make eye contact with the new prisoners, but on this occasion, he made an exception. He motioned to Rachel not to make any gestures to him.

When they were standing close to each other, she managed to whisper, "I know what they are going to do to us. We heard about this place."

Quickly and carefully, she took a sock from her bag containing diamonds and placed it in his cupped hands. "Stay safe and may G-d bless you." With her last words, Rachel received the finger gesture to line up on the gas chamber line. Mondig's last human contact with his Warsaw past was shortly reduced to ashes.

The SS guard noticed Mondig had stopped working. He admonished Mondig, whipped him, and demanded he work faster.

While piling the suitcases onto the truck, Mondig noticed the dreadful Herr Schilinger appear on the scene. Schilinger strutted, a club in one hand, ready to pounce at a second's notice. The Nazi stared at a beautiful woman among the prisoners. Mondig watched him as he walked over to her and put his arms around her, attempting to kiss her. Unbeknownst to Schilinger, she had a gun hidden in her clothes. She reached for her gun and shot him in the chest.

All hell broke out. Guards ran from all directions, sirens went off, and the vicious dogs attacked. Mondig grabbed the suitcases and scurried back to the Canada warehouse. He didn't see what happened to the woman, but he could only guess.

When he arrived at the Canada, he noticed all the other workers were diligently working, minding their own business. Mondig saw a large, odd-looking suitcase on a table. He opened it quickly, as by now he was a master of breaking open locks. His eyes sparkled and his heart pounded. He couldn't believe what he saw—right before his eyes were rolls and rolls of bills, liquor, cigarettes, and diamonds. Unfortunately, he had no place to hide the liquor and cigarettes, but he took as many of the bills and diamonds as he could conceal on his person. He slipped out of the warehouse and walked briskly to the back of bunker 26. He buried his newly acquired treasures.

I am sure someday these treasures will bring me, and hopefully others, our freedom. Maybe a miracle will happen.

Winter was approaching. Everyone dreaded the frigid winter as it brought additional deaths. In addition to the cruelty initiated by the Nazis, mother nature brought fierce winds, freezing temperatures, rain, and snow. Prisoners were not given warmer clothes to wear. There were many days Mondig and the others were forced to walk in the pouring rain wearing wooden clogs, stumbling in the mud.

The grounds of Birkenau kept growing to accommodate continued masses of transports. The winter of 1944 brought even more transports. On January 30, 1944, 700 Jews arrived from Milan, Italy. February 8, 1944, brought 1,015 Jews from Holland. 2,000 Jews arrived from Hungary in May 1944. Auschwitz-Birkenau became the site of the largest mass murder center in history.

Mondig had limited contact with the new arrivals. The longtime prisoners were separated from the new ones. He surmised from the number of prisoners and the growth of Birkenau that the Nazis were conquering and continuing to expand. He saw more electrical barbed-wired fences and more barracks. Approximately

2,000 guards were now patrolling, and the number of suitcases to sort through increased.

Despite it all, Mondig felt blessed to be alive. He had a decent relationship with some Nazi guards and Jewish *kapos*. However, he wondered how long his good fortune would last and when his time would expire, too.

Will I go up in flames as well, or will my body just fail? Will I survive? Does anyone survive Hell? What will be my ultimate fate?

Both psychologically and physically, he neared exhaustion. Witnessing brutality every day for several years took its toll. Every minute alive tested his will. He had recurring nightmares of a scene from the selection ramp. As a woman exited the train holding onto her infant, a Nazi demanded she release her child and let him walk alone. It was obvious the child was no older than six months and could not walk.

The woman refused to let go of her child. The Nazi violently yanked him from the mother's tight grip and screamed, "Walk."

The infant fell to the ground. The officer picked up the infant and threw him in the air, proclaiming, "If you can't walk, you will fly."

With those words, he shot the baby. Everyone stood paralyzed as the remains of the infant splattered on the ground. The mother fainted and received the same fate—a shot in the head.

Mondig knew he could only desensitize himself so much. He longed to hear babies laugh and see mothers hold their children again. He wanted to be free, to wear clean clothes, to eat real food, and to laugh, but most of all he didn't want to see innocent people being murdered. He had to find a way out of this Hell. He had tried before and failed, but he had to attempt again, although he knew it couldn't be from Birkenau. An escape from Birkenau was virtually impossible. He had to get transferred to another camp. Four years was enough for him!

I must get out of here. I can't be a slave to these animals anymore. I want my life back. I don't want my life to revolve around someone's whims. I want to be a free man.

A Polish Guard officer named Viktor walked through the campgrounds twice a day for surveillance purposes. Amazingly, he sometimes even told jokes to the prisoners. He differed from the other Nazis. Mondig thought Viktor might be his key to a successful transfer.

During one of Viktor's rounds, Mondig approached him. "Viktor, I want to talk to you, one Polish soldier to another—man to man."

They agreed to speak in Viktor's office in the Canada warehouse at 4:00 p.m. that day. Nervously, Mondig entered the office and noticed a picture of Adolf Hitler hanging above the desk. The Nazi flag with the swastika hung in the corner of the room.

Viktor looked perplexed by the request of a Jewish prisoner to speak to an SS guard.

"Who is this fearless Jew who is willing to take the risk to talk to me? Is he not scared of me?" Viktor probably asked himself.

"Viktor, I was a high-ranking soldier in the Polish army. You are also a soldier. Let us forget for a moment we are fighting in a war, and let's talk man to man. You are aware of my job sorting goods."

Mondig knew he could be shot at any moment, but he took the risk.

"Go on," Viktor replied curiously.

"I've come across valuables that would make your eyes pop out. I know it is just as illegal for you to take them as it was for me to steal them. However, if you want, I will be happy to give them to you, and you will be a wealthy man." Mondig was trembling.

Is Viktor going to pounce on me and shoot me between the eyes or will he be interested?

Mondig knew his life was endangered, but he was also aware that Viktor would not get the valuables if he killed Mondig. He hoped that Viktor would realize that it would be in his best interest not to kill him. And luckily, he did.

"Obviously, you want something in return? You are not giving a Nazi officer anything out of the kindness of your heart. What makes you trust that I won't force you to give me all your valuables and then shoot you?" inquired Viktor.

"Could happen, but I don't think you would do that. You would always want more, and I will be your source of wealth. Let's work out a plan that is mutually beneficial," Mondig said, trying to negotiate.

"Does anyone else know about this?" Viktor questioned.

"No. I didn't tell anyone. You are the only one who knows." Mondig was delighted that Viktor expressed an interest in his proposition. "I approached you because I have a feeling you are a good man and we can work together."

"Good. Keep it that way. What exactly do you have?" Viktor continued. Mondig was pleased with Viktor's interest. He only told him about the bills and money, neglecting to mention other valuables he had.

"We have to formulate a solid plan. If you get caught, you will be shot. If I get caught, I will also be shot for taking stolen property. Let me think for a second." Viktor paused. "I will give you a small briefcase with an envelope inside. Put the money in the envelope. When you go to work tomorrow at the Canada, you will pretend you are taking the suitcase to sort through the possessions. I will meet you behind the warehouse. One word of caution. If you get caught, do not mention my name. I do not know you. If you mention my name, I will kill you. Understood? Now, what do you want in return?"

Mondig didn't have to hesitate to answer and blurted out the words, "Get me out of Birkenau."

Viktor was puzzled as to the reason Mondig wanted a transfer, because working in the Canada warehouse seemed to be an ideal assignment. Viktor didn't know of a better place to work.

* * *

Before they concluded the conversation, an announcement blared from the loudspeaker. "Prisoner number 31321 report to Commandant Krieg immediately."

Apparently, someone reported that Mondig was missing. "Viktor, that's my number. I'm in deep trouble."

"Don't worry. I can take care of that," Viktor reassured him. With that, Viktor made a phone call and then in a matter of minutes replied to Mondig, "You are safe. You do not have to report to the commandant."

Once again, Mondig had straddled the narrow line between life and death. The next obstacle was getting the money to Viktor.

Will the plan work?

Luckily, the plan went undetected, and Viktor became wealthy with the valuables Mondig gave him. The next morning, Mondig was summoned to the courtyard.

CHAPTER 12

Next Stop—Sachsenhausen Concentration Camp

SS Schwartzhue pointed to Mondig and asked, "You are 31321?"

Why are you asking such a stupid question? You know my number, Mondig laughed to himself.

Mondig replied with fright, "Jawohl."

"You are a *Schlossmacher*, a mechanic, right?" asked Schwartzhue. "*Jawohl!*" Mondig lied, afraid to admit that he didn't know the first thing about mechanics.

"You are being transferred to Sachsenhausen with 1,500 other inmates to work in an airplane factory."

Did Viktor, the Polish guard, really help me?

Mondig was thrilled to be leaving Birkenau. The long-awaited day finally came. On November 2, 1944,

Mondig joyfully said his final farewells to Auschwitz–Birkenau—never to look back.

No sooner had he arrived at Sachsenhausen camp, north of Berlin, Germany, a German officer from Auschwitz recognized him and said, "You are not a mechanic. You are a swine *Jude*. Jews are not permitted to work in the airplane factory."

His assignment changed. He was given a long pole with a metal point on the end and was instructed to walk the grounds, picking up the trash and depositing it in a tall receptacle. Mondig accepted this task and looked forward to walking outside in the fresh air and stretching his legs.

This camp differed from Auschwitz–Birkenau. Although life in Sachsenhausen was also barbaric, it wasn't quite as harsh as what Mondig had already experienced. A wall and electric fence surrounded the camp. 400 inmates shared seven toilets. The roll call took place in a semicircular space where they stood in the morning and the evening.

Most of all, Mondig appreciated the absence of Dr. Mengele and his selection ramp. Despite still feeling surrounded by death, it didn't have the same constant odor of dead bodies, which Mondig loathed. Inmates were brought in, worked, suffered, and passed out from exhaustion and disease. Mondig still held onto his will to live. He never stopped thinking about his family and prayed to G-d that by some miracle, he would see them again.

Prisoners arrived in droves in late 1944. Rumors circulated that the Soviet Army was advancing and the Nazis were attempting to get prisoners out of Auschwitz and move them west. Mondig wondered if that explained why he was transferred there or, if indeed, it was due to Viktor's influence. At that point, it didn't matter. The only thing that mattered was that he was out of Auschwitz-Birkenau. News came that the American and British armies were trying to stop the Germans.

Is the outside world finally coming to our aid? Did the world finally wake up?

Mondig wondered what took them so long but was grateful they might be nearing.

On November 17, 1944, Mondig had yet another transfer, this time to Dachau concentration camp. He never knew why he was transferred, but later was glad he was. This was his lifeline.

Dachau was the first concentration camp opened in 1933, and it was situated north of Munich, Germany. Mondig remembered hearing about it being used as a political reeducation camp, but found out that it had other purposes.

CHAPTER 13

Is Escape from Dachau Concentration Camp Possible?

Dachau, similar to other concentration camps, was surrounded by barbed wire and long, deep ditches. Rows of approximately 30 symmetrical, narrow barracks covered the pebbled grounds, and gas chambers lay at the northern end. The barracks were not heated and were frigid during the German winters. Mondig's barrack consisted of two rooms, one used as a day room and the other a night room. Sanitary conditions were as terrible as in the other camps, and many people died from dysentery and other illnesses. The tower was constantly manned by a guard pointing a machine gun at the inmates. Mondig was sent to Lager 11, where he joined 7,000 other prisoners.

Although there were two crematoriums, the stench of dead humans wasn't as strong as in Birkenau. Nothing compared to Birkenau.

Upon arrival, Mondig was given a different uniform to wear with a yellow star patch and a new number to remember. Mondig quickly was informed of the rules of the new camp. The punishments for defiance included standing still for hours and food deprivation. None of this was new to Mondig. He was all too familiar with the deadly routine. After all, he had been a prisoner since 1939.

* * *

The inmates at Dachau knew of the Allies' advance and shared the information with each other. However, even though the Allies were advancing, Mondig knew he must try to escape once again. The timing was right. He knew his body couldn't withstand much more abuse. He also worried about what further atrocities the Nazis might commit as the Allies got closer.

Will the Nazis kill everyone before the Allies come? Will they want to destroy the "evidence" of their brutal acts?

Is Escape from Dachau Concentration Camp Possible?

There were many subcamps at Dachau, and some of the prisoners served as slave laborers for the camps. One day he was sent to work assisting a blacksmith at one of the camp's factories. For some odd reason, the blacksmith left him alone for a few minutes when he went to the bathroom. Mondig noticed a pair of pliers on the ground, and he immediately took them and concealed them in his pants, thinking they might come to good use. When he returned to the barracks, he ripped a hole in the straw mattress and hid the pliers in it, next to the diamonds that he smuggled from Auschwitz. Mondig had become an expert thief.

How will I escape? Is escape from Dachau possible?

CHAPTER 14

A New and Unlikely Friendship

Mondig spoke with some of the older prisoners, and they agreed that something seemed different. It was early 1945, and they noticed the Germans were burning many boxes that seemed to contain papers.

Are they burning evidence? What are they doing?

The guards were acting peculiar. They seemed to be covering many things they were carrying and whispering much of the time. At other times, they meandered with no specific purpose.

Mondig didn't understand the changes. Were they good or bad?

He prayed the war was coming to an end. *Is there a chance it is over? Please, G-d. Let it end.*

The uncertainty bothered Mondig because he wasn't sure how to react. He had already decided the timing was right to plan his final escape, but he wasn't certain how to execute it, considering the new developments. He would have to figure it out.

Mondig always remembered the first time he met Rudy. He was over six feet tall, muscular, and strikingly handsome. His blue eyes sparkled, and his long blond hair gave him a distinguished look. He periodically came to Dachau to get workers for his lumberyard, the *Firma Rachel*, a subcamp, situated on the outskirts of Dachau camp. On one occasion, Rudy sent Mondig to work there.

Mondig and Rudy developed a friendship, which was odd, as Rudy was a German Nazi and Mondig was a Polish Jew. As strange as it was, Rudy took a liking to Mondig. He told Mondig he admired him for his bravery and his willingness to face adversity head on – something Rudy could never do.

Often during a break, they sat together and conversed, sharing their experiences. Mondig told Rudy about his family and his past imprisonments.

Rudy was shocked to hear what Mondig had lived through. It seemed impossible that he had survived all the torture. He was moved by Mondig's determination to live.

"What gave you the strength to live? How did you survive the beatings?" Rudy would inquire. Rudy had never been to Auschwitz and was curious to hear about it from a Jew.

Mondig sensed that Rudy was different from the other Nazis he had encountered. He was sensitive and seemed human. He enjoyed his conversations with Rudy and looked forward to seeing him.

Rudy told Mondig about how he became a Nazi soldier and later a high-ranking SS officer. "I never really thought twice about becoming an officer. I knew it was expected of me. I was scared that refusing to do so would have meant death to my family and me. Just as you did things to save yourself and your family, I did the same. I grew up in a strict family and accepted orders without questioning my elders. I was an obedient son and devoted soldier."

Mondig was curious. "Do you hate Jews?"

"I don't hate them. I don't think about them. I just do as I am told," responded Rudy.

In some strange way, Mondig could understand those words. At the time, everyone had to fend for himself and do what he could to survive.

And that's what Mondig wanted to do. He thought about Bruno, the Nazi from Auschwitz, and how he was able to bribe him with chocolate and how he bribed Viktor with money. He remembered all the others who succumbed to bribery and trickery. Bribes seemed to work well with the SS. Maybe he could be Rudy's supplier of stolen goods as well. When Mondig offered Rudy the same deal, not surprisingly, Rudy gracefully accepted his offer.

* * *

Mondig still wrestled about the morality of what he was doing.

Is surviving through bribery acceptable? Am I committing a crime?

Justifying his actions, he knew if he didn't do it, he too would be murdered. He felt he had the right to try everything possible to live. What point would dying serve? Mondig knew survivors were needed—strong people who could tell the world exactly what happened. It was a matter of life and death. Maybe G-d had given him strength to survive and in the future, deliver the awful truth to the world.

"Mondig, there is a transport coming in tonight, and I'm sure there will be a considerable amount of valuable goods locked in the train before being shipped to Berlin. Do you think you can get them?" Mondig had no idea how he was going to accomplish this feat, but he dared not defy his new friend, Rudy.

"What do you want me to do?" asked Mondig curiously.

Mondig did not feel comfortable in his new surroundings. He knew Auschwitz like the back of his hand, as he helped build it. However, Dachau was foreign land for him. But he also knew he had to win Rudy's trust.

"This is the plan. I have the keys to the last car of the train. You will load the lumber on the train. They need the lumber to be shipped to Berlin. I will send my assistant, Gruber, to help you load the lumber with 20 other prisoners. You will meet him there. Gruber will be told to save several pieces of broken lumber for you. You will break the lock in the next car, take out some goods for me, and place them between the broken pieces of lumber in the wagon. Gruber will tell the guards we are returning the lumber to the camp because they are not in adequate condition to be sent to Berlin."

Mondig didn't like the plan. It sounded too dangerous. However, he didn't have a choice. He had to trust Rudy and assume Rudy thought the plan would work. He liked Rudy and needed to form an alliance with him.

The next Monday, Mondig met Gruber outside the train as planned. Gruber opened the car, placed the lumber in it, and told Mondig, "The rest is up to you."

Mondig broke the lock of the second car and quickly went inside. He looked around, making certain nobody was watching him. He was shocked by all the chocolate, liquor, cigars, leather coats, and valuables he saw. It reminded him of the day in the Canada warehouse in Auschwitz when he opened the suitcase and found a mint of treasures.

Can I be so lucky? Is G-d helping me?

Mondig seized the valuables and placed them on the wagon. He didn't tell Gruber about the *extras* he managed to hide and keep for himself. Mondig and Gruber pushed the wagon to Rudy's office. Rudy got what he wanted, and Mondig got an unexpected reward. Both parties were satisfied.

A few days later, Rudy congratulated Mondig on a successful task and asked him if he could repeat it. The following week, Gruber and Mondig repeated the heist, this time adding jewelry and coats to their take.

Of course, Rudy was pleased with the *thief* he discovered, and Mondig became Rudy's path to wealth. Rudy assured Mondig, "If I can ever help you, let me know. We are friends."

Those words resonated with Mondig; he did not know if they were sincere, but he stored them in his memory.

Will a Nazi really help me? Am I really friends with a German Nazi? The next day, Mondig was instructed to report to an office building. A high-ranking officer spoke to Rudy and informed him that he needed men to carry furniture to his new office. For Mondig, it was a stroke of good luck. As Mondig was transporting a bookcase into the *offizier*'s office, he noticed a shiny object on a chair. He inched closer to get a clearer look and discovered it was a gun belt suspended from a chair.

It was unimaginable.

A gun within reach with nobody near me!

Without giving it a second thought, he unbuckled the holster, grabbed the gun, and hid it in his pants. Mondig knew he would be killed if caught, but he was willing to take the risk. When he returned to the barracks, he hid the gun next to the pliers in the straw mattress. He had to quickly decide what his next step would be, because the clock was rapidly ticking.

CHAPTER 15

First One In, Last One Out

Mondig was excited. He had buried all the essentials for an escape: diamonds, a gun, and pliers, along with the promise of a German Nazi to assist him, as absurd as it sounded. Mondig realized the time to attempt another escape was ripe. He was very anxious about what the Nazis would do to the prisoners as the Allies approached the camp, and knew he had to get out of there.

It is now or never.

He turned to another prisoner, Marik Samolevich, a Polish Jew, whom he had befriended in Auschwitz.

"Marik, we must escape. The Germans will not let the Allies find us alive." Mondig put it in simple words. It didn't take much to convince Marik.

Mondig swore that G-d was watching over him because at that precise moment, they could hear the drone of planes overhead, and an air-raid alert went off. G-d had answered his prayers. All the lights in the camp were turned off. It was pitch black. Mondig's escape could not have been timed better.

Without faltering, Mondig commanded, "Let's go."

Mondig quickly dug up the diamonds, gun, and pliers that he had carefully hidden. He and Marik dashed to the barbed-wire fence. As the lights were off, they knew there was no electricity, so they didn't worry about being electrocuted.

As they were cutting the wire on the fence with the pliers Mondig had stolen, an officer approached them. Mondig grabbed the officer's neck and put his gun to the officer's head and shot him. Marik quickly removed the officer's gun from the holster.

As Mondig looked up at the watchtower, he noticed another officer with his back to him. Mondig didn't wait a second. Without hesitation, he shot the officer.

Lucky I was a Polish soldier and know how to use a gun.

With all the chaos over the lack of electricity, nobody heard the gunshots. Mondig climbed the tower and undressed the German soldier. He dressed himself in the guard's Nazi uniform. Mondig was now dressed as a Nazi SS officer. Mondig grabbed the dead officer's gun and ran down the watchtower.

Mondig instructed Marik, "You walk in front of me. I will act as a Nazi officer. I will point my gun at you. If we are stopped, I will say you are my prisoner." There was no time to think. They had to act quickly.

With all the turmoil, the loud noise of the airplanes flying above them, the power failure, and the mass confusion, Mondig and Marik marched through the gates of Dachau concentration camp, with Mondig acting as a German soldier. They soon found themselves standing on the outside of Dachau.

We did it!

Mondig's wish had come true. He had survived the heinous acts of the Nazis and walked out of Dachau on his own terms. The Nazis failed to dispose of him through the chimney in Auschwitz–Birkenau. Mondig was among the first in and the last out of the concentration camps. He was the sole survivor of the original eight Jews who entered Auschwitz.

What next?

CHAPTER 16
The Ditch

Mondig and Marik walked away from the camp, holding their breath with every step they took, never looking back. Rudy once told Mondig where he lived and described his house. Luckily, it was close to the camp and easy to locate.

Mondig's unexpected arrival at the house would be the ultimate test to determine if Rudy's promise to help him was a bluff or sincere.

Are we really friends or just partners in crime?

Mondig and Marik finally arrived at Rudy's house, uncertain of the reception they would receive.

Mondig told Marik to hide in the bushes. "If all goes well, I'll call you. If you hear gunshots, run."

Mondig approached the door, trembling. He knocked. This really was the moment of truth. What lay in store for them on the other side of the door?

How is Rudy going to respond? Will he help me, as he promised he would? What is my fate? My life is now in Rudy's hands.

The window on the second floor opened slightly, and a man peeked out at Mondig. It was not Rudy. Mondig did not recognize him. Mondig stiffened but responded by raising his right arm in the Nazi salute of allegiance. "Heil Hitler." Mondig's knowledge of languages and his ability to speak with a German accent came in handy.

The man responded in German. "Who are you? Why are you waking me up in the middle of the night? Did something happen?"

"I am here to see Rudy. It is important. He will understand," Mondig explained.

In a few minutes, the front door opened, and Mondig entered. Clad in a German uniform, Mondig stood at attention and once again gave the infamous salute, "Heil Hitler."

The German led Mondig to the living room, where he saw Rudy sprawled out on the couch. Mondig couldn't believe how beautiful the house was. He hadn't seen such gorgeous furniture since he was in his own home in Warsaw. He wanted to run over to the dining room table and grab the cognac or reach for the fresh fruit. It seemed surreal to him.

Rudy was dumfounded to see Mondig and inquired, "How did you get here? Why are you dressed in an SS guard's uniform? What is going on? I am so happy to see you, but tell me how you got here." Before Mondig could answer, Rudy got up and hugged Mondig.

At that point, Mondig knew Rudy was going to keep his word and help him.

What a relief!

Mondig explained briefly about his escape and told Rudy about Marik hiding outside.

"Bring your friend inside," Rudy instructed Mondig.

Mondig didn't need to be told again. He quickly went outside and got him.

As they stood in the living room, Mondig stared at the strange man who had initially opened the front door for him. Something didn't feel right. The man was staring at Mondig and seemed uneasy. Rudy introduced him as his nephew.

After a brief conversation, Rudy turned to his nephew and instructed him to hide Mondig and his friend Marik in the cellar. At this point, the petrified nephew refused. "Are you crazy? If we get caught hiding escaped Jews, we will all be killed. Why would you risk our lives for two Jews? What's wrong with you, Uncle? The SS will be looking for them. I won't do it."

Rudy pleaded. "These men are different. Mondig is my friend. He is a good man."

His pleading fell on deaf ears. The nephew would not be an accomplice to hiding Jews.

Upon hearing the commotion, Rudy's brother entered the room and immediately agreed with his son. "Get them out of here, and the sooner the better. You have gone crazy, Rudy. If you don't get them out, I will, and it won't be pleasant."

At this point, Rudy and Mondig knew that further pleas would be in vain. "Don't worry, Mondig. I am a man of my word. I promised to help you, and I will. It took such strength and ingenuity to escape Dachau.

I am not going to let you down now. Not after all you have been through."

With that, Rudy grabbed a bag of food, a blanket, and shovels. They walked about three kilometers in the dark until they saw a sign—"*Eintritt Verboten* [Entry Forbidden]." They ignored the sign, cut the barbed wire, and proceeded cautiously. Then Rudy advised Mondig of their dangerous predicament. This was an old, deserted farm, off the path from the SS guards. However, there was one man living in a guardhouse not too far from where they were standing.

"Mondig and Marik, listen carefully. Do you see that little house over there? We have one obstacle now. Inside is an old German man guarding what was once his farm. He is frail, and senile, but he has a gun. Every day he goes out with his gun, protecting what he thinks belongs to him. In order to be safe, you must kill him. I promised to help you, and I will—but I won't kill a fellow German. You go in, do what you have do, don't tell me, and I will wait here," Rudy instructed.

It seemed strange, but Mondig and Marik didn't ask any questions. They knew what had to be done. This was an easy task compared to what they had already endured. They accomplished their goal without any incident and quickly returned to Rudy. They never spoke about it.

The three men continued trekking across the open land. Mondig and Rudy plowed ahead and did not notice that Marik failed to keep pace. When Mondig asked Marik a question without receiving a response, he turned around; Marik was lying motionless on the ground. He hadn't heard any gunshots and hadn't seen anyone. Mondig bent over his friend's body and knew instantly that Marik had reached his end. His body just couldn't hold out any longer. Mondig's only sense of relief was that a Nazi hadn't killed his friend. He died on his own terms, outside the grounds of Dachau. Mondig wanted to give him a proper burial, unlike all the other Jews who were denied their final resting rights.

They dug a hole and slowly lowered his body inside while Mondig recited the familiar mourner's prayer, "*Yitgadal, Vyitkadash…*" as he wept uncontrollably.

Marik was so close to a new life. Mondig had hoped that he and Marik would regain their freedom together. It didn't happen. Mondig was by himself.

Not too far from the makeshift grave, Mondig and Rudy dug another hole—this one for Mondig—the ditch Mondig ended up hiding in for 12 days and ultimately collapsing in.

CHAPTER 17

The Americans Arrive —April 29, 1945

"Töte ihn [Kill him]!"

Unidentifiable voices woke Mondig from his stupor. He opened his eyes, but still in a state of delirium, he thought he heard Nazis screaming, "Kill the *Jude!*"

He wasn't completely sure of his surroundings yet.

Where am I? Who am I? What year is it?

The sounds got louder. It sounded like people were screaming in German and dogs howling.

As Mondig's senses returned and he regained his cognition, he realized he might be in trouble and tried to bury himself deeper into the ditch. He remembered the events leading to the present—the years of abuse, his escape, his hiding in the ditch, and his friend Rudy.

Who is hovering overhead? What voices do I hear? Do I hear dogs howling? Are the Nazis coming to get me? I need Rudy now.

Mondig knew the dogs from Dachau would salivate at the smell of a human and would jump at the opportunity to rip his body to shreds.

After a few minutes, he was able to hear the sounds clearer. They were not dogs barking. What he heard was the human voice.

Suddenly, to Mondig's delight, he knew the words he heard weren't German. He heard people speaking in English! Mondig looked up and to his utter delight he saw American soldiers standing directly above him, surrounding the perimeter of the ditch.

The Americans lifted him out of the ditch, threw him on the ground, encircled him and pointed their guns at him.

"Hands up!"

"Don't shoot. I'm a Jew. I'm a Jew," Mondig kept reiterating, although it took every effort on his part to get the words out. By now, Mondig looked and felt like a walking skeleton, wearing a drenched Nazi uniform full of body excretions. The Americans maintained their position, circling him with guns directly pointed at him, and repeated, "You are no Jew."

Mondig realized that, dressed in a Nazi uniform, the Americans thought he was a Nazi. Mondig knew he couldn't die now, especially at the hands of Americans, but he had no strength to continue to talk or to explain why he was wearing a Nazi's uniform. By some streak of luck, in his last minutes of a fierce struggle for his life, he had an idea. With all his strength, he pulled up the left sleeve on his stolen Nazi uniform and revealed the number forever tattooed on his arm—31321.

Struggling to breathe, he slowly and carefully said, "Look at my arm. I am a Polish Jew."

And with those last words, he gasped for air.

The Americans assisted him getting up, hugged and kissed him. Suddenly, he heard someone speaking Yiddish! He wanted to scream for joy. It was a man named Captain Kirschbaum, a Jew, from New York. This was the happiest moment Mondig had in so many years. It was April 29, 1945. Mondig had spent almost six years in prisons, concentration camps, and hiding in an underground ditch for 12 days.

I am finally free! I did it! I survived!

April 29, 1945 was a day full of extreme emotion for Mondig.

> *April 29, 1945 is the greatest day in my life. April 29, 1945 is the day I was reborn.*

> *April 29, 1945 is the day I regained my freedom. Freedom, at last!*

Mondig was taken to a house that was designated as the Jewish Recovery House (coincidentally, it was built using the lumber from Rudy's lumberyard) and stayed there to recuperate.

The US Seventh Army's 45th Infantry Division liberated Dachau the same day the Americans found Mondig, and all the inmates at the camp were set free. No more beatings. No more killings. No more starvation. The brutality was finally over.

The next day, April 30, 1945, brought more good news: Adolf Hitler killed himself by gunshot. Adolf Hitler was dead! When Mondig heard the news, he cried and cried. He cried for the lives lost, for the lives that never were, and for the attempted destruction of mankind. Other liberated Jewish prisoners were brought to the Recovery House. They looked like ghastly skeletons and obviously needed a great deal of medical attention. They were given chocolate, food, drinks, shelter, and beds with clean linen. Sadly, some survivors died from overeating as their sick bodies couldn't digest the food. A doctor treating Mondig told him he couldn't believe he was still alive after all the attacks on his body. He had numerous scars all over his body, not to mention the disfigurations and broken bones throughout. He had lost 80 pounds, and he was no longer the handsome, muscular man he had been almost six years earlier. He was nothing more than skin and bones with sunken cheeks. But he didn't care; he was alive and on the way to recovery.

His life started to change. For the first time in years, Mondig looked in a mirror. He was shocked at what he saw.

That can't possibly be me.

Slowly, he began to get some normality back in his life. Fond memories started to fill Mondig's heart. The laughter of children echoed in his mind. His family. His hometown of Warsaw. He began to laugh and smile again. He ate decent food. He made friends. He began to become human again.

On May 3, General Eisenhower visited the Recovery House. He promised the survivors that the Americans would take care of them, which indeed they did. Captain Kirschbaum appointed Mondig the *mayor* of the house.

On May 8, 1945, Germany surrendered to the Allies, and this time Mondig and his friends celebrated with their own bottle of cognac, not a confiscated one.

Mondig slowly got his strength back, and a few months later, he further recuperated at a Displaced Persons Camp (DP camp) in Epfenhausen, Germany. He arrived at the camp with no family, no job, and no home. However, he had the most important things life could offer him—the hope of starting a new life and fulfilling his dream of telling the world what really happened.

CHAPTER 18

A Witness at the Nuremberg Trials

Many Nazi leaders were captured after the war. The United States and Great Britain demanded fair trials for them and selected Nuremberg, Germany, as the location. The trials lasted from November 1945 until October 1949. The accused were tried for four categories of crimes—conspiracy to commit crimes, crimes against peace, war crimes, and crimes against humanity.

At the request of the American government, Mondig was sent to Nuremberg to bear witness at one of the trials. He, of course, knew many of the accused Nazis because he had been in the camps longer than most inmates. He witnessed Auschwitz grow from swamps into an empire, where over one million Jews were brutally murdered. He spent six weeks testifying against the accused.

As Mondig sat in a witness box, the judge asked him to identify himself.

"I was born Moishe Scheinberg. In the concentration camps, I was known as Mondig until the Nazis took away my name and replaced it with number 31321. I was given the name Morris at the DP camp. As you see, I am a man of many names."

"What camps were you in? When were you first taken to the camps? When were you liberated?"

When the judge heard that Morris had been forcibly taken from his home in 1939 and that he had survived the camps and escaped in 1945, his face paled. "My goodness. You survived a very, very long time. You are a hero. You must know many of the defendants."

Morris confirmed, "Yes, I was one of the first of eight Jews sent to Auschwitz from Tarnow, Poland. Of those eight Jews, I was the only one to survive. You are correct, Your Honor. I came across many Nazis during that time."

The judge looked bewildered. "Look at the defendants and tell me if you can identify anyone."

Morris took a deep breath, choked on his tears, and pointed to one of the accused. "That man led Jews to the showers at Auschwitz." The questions came quickly. They weren't easy to address and demanded that Morris revisit the heinous acts he witnessed and brutal life he endured.

Perspiration continued to drip from his forehead. He paused and had to take a sip of water. The horrors of the past stared directly into his face as he saw horrible, inhuman creatures sitting in front of him.

Will the pain ever go away? Can I ever forget what happened?

"Do you want to take a break?" asked the judge, sensing Morris was upset.

Morris knew he had lived for this minute, although he was not sure he could answer all the questions that brought back such horrible memories. He had to regain his confidence.

Tell the world what I saw. I have waited for this moment for a very long time. Tell the world…

With that, Morris replied to the judge, "No, I do not need a break."

One by one, he named the Nazis he knew. He testified against 10 former SS defendants. He now was up to the 11th defendant. The defendant looked familiar but had a different name. He was thinner and older looking than what Morris remembered, but when Morris and he made eye contact, Morris knew instantly.

He's my friend Rudy.

Morris jumped out of his seat, barely able to contain himself. He was shocked. Rudy was sitting directly across from him. Rudy must have recognized him as well, because tears rolled down his cheeks.

They both were visibly shaken. Morris gasped. He wanted to run up to his long-lost friend. He wanted to hug him and tell him how much he missed him and how grateful he was for what he did.

After a few seconds, Morris spoke. "That man over there is Rudy. I know him from Dachau. I am aware he was a German Nazi, and I know he was a high-ranking officer in Dachau and owned a lumber factory that used Jewish prisoners for hard labor. I am also aware that he probably did some things he shouldn't have done. However, I can only say, if it weren't for him, I wouldn't be here to tell my story. He risked his life to save mine."

A Witness at the Nuremberg Trials

In the end, a German Nazi saved a Polish Jew, and in return, the Polish Jew saved the German Nazi.

CHAPTER 19

A New Life in
the United States

Morris returned to the DP camp and met another survivor, Sonya Beder, who was also from Warsaw, Poland. He and Sonya married on May 8, 1946. Life was not easy for either of them after they were liberated. They were alone, with no livelihood and no family.

Luckily, they were awarded assistance from a Jewish agency and were sent to Landsberg, Germany, where they waited for the American immigration quota to grant them permission to enter the United States. While many of the survivors wanted to go to Palestine (which became the State of Israel in 1948), Morris wanted to go to America—the country who ultimately saved him. While waiting for their visa, they visited their hometown of Warsaw, only to find a destroyed city. Morris's house and business were gone. There was no evidence they ever existed. In fact, Warsaw had no resemblance at all to the one they grew up in. Morris's entire past was erased as if it never happened.

Morris and Sonya were thrilled to leave Germany on April 24, 1947, and moved to the new life awaiting them in Los Angeles, California. They came to the United States empty-handed, with only one piece of memorabilia from Morris's past: a very small picture of himself as a soldier in the Polish army.

Morris again assumed a new name, but this time it was one of his choosing. In America, he wanted to be called Murray. He deserved a new name, for a new life, in a new country. He wanted to rid himself of the vestiges of his awful past.

Murray worked at various administrative jobs in Los Angeles but was unsuccessful. So, he decided to try his luck at the only profession he knew from his former life in Warsaw—business. He opened several types of businesses, and although not as successful as in Warsaw, he managed to do well. He retired in 1962.

* * *

Although a free man, the ghosts of his life under the Third Reich haunted him until the day he died. Almost every night, he woke up screaming from reoccurring nightmares of scenes from his disturbing past.

Why did they kill my family? Why did they kill others?

Murray was emotionally scarred. The war had taken its toll on him, and he could not relinquish his role as a *victim*. Murray was unable to free himself of the horror he had experienced. He couldn't forgive himself for not leaving Poland with his family. He blamed himself for his family's peril. He searched for reasons for his own survival.

Murray never fully understood why G-d chose him to live. He felt that he had survived for one reason—to fulfill a dream in passing history and knowledge to future generations. Time was moving forward, and the world had to know. It had to be reminded of the painful truth. Murray dedicated the rest of his life to sharing the dreadful horrors he and millions of other innocent Jews experienced. He spoke to people at parks, lectured at libraries and schools, and disclosed the terrifying experiences that shaped his life and millions of others.

Never again can or will this happen!

* * *

Murray often wondered what happened to Rudy. In fact, he tried to locate him through the German consulate and embassy but failed. He wished he could see him again.

Sadly, after a rocky 21 years of marriage, Murray and Sonya got divorced. The past was too heavy on both their hearts to enable them to stay together forever.

After the divorce, Murray continued to harbor profound hate toward the German Nazis and remained a prisoner within himself. He could not extricate himself from the insanity and heartless brutality he endured during the Holocaust.

How can I forget the barbaric killings I witnessed or the brutal attacks I suffered for almost six years?

There was no escaping the awful memories.

* * *

As his anger and hatred lingered, his fate luckily changed, and he met his third love—my Aunt Rose, an American Jewish divorcée. Aunt Rose brought her own share of problems into the marriage—having been the victim of an abusive husband in a previous marriage, and having to raise a severely asthmatic child by herself. Additionally, she had serious medical conditions. However, Aunt Rose and Uncle Murray were perfect for each other as they complemented each other in every way.

When my family and I visited them, Uncle Murray repeatedly revealed his ugly past to me and my brothers, unembarrassed to show us his frightening scars. Often, out of the blue, he would have a flashback and start to rant in Polish, German, Yiddish, and English, spewing venom against the Nazis.

We saw his knife marks, the wounds in his head, his distorted bones, and the number on his arm—31321. Uncle Murray never forgave the German Nazis or their collaborators for what they did.

"How can I forgive animals who killed my family and attempted to kill every Jew in Europe? How can I forgive vicious, brutal people who got pleasure out of causing others agonizing pain? And how can I forgive people who thrived on stealing my last breath of life? Is that what forgiveness is?" my uncle asked me.

I had no answer.

As he visibly got upset, my Aunt Rose calmed him in her soft, tranquil voice. "Don't worry, Murray. It's OK. Don't get upset. It's in the past." Rose had a magic touch with Murray. When Murray indulged in a violent tirade against the Nazis, she lovingly brought him back to reality, offering him support and comfort. She was able to bring peace into his otherwise shattered life.

Despite it all, Murray kept some perspective. He also had a magic touch with Rose. Once the anti-Nazi venom subsided, a warm man reemerged. All the horrors did not kill Murray's core of decency. He gave Rose his undivided love and took care of her. He injected her with daily insulin and took her to her numerous doctor appointments. He did the shopping and cleaning. He devoted himself to her as if he had no inner turmoil at all. And she devoted herself to him.

During our conversations, he told us that although many people refer to the "six" million Jews murdered during the Holocaust, he knew the number was incorrect. He was certain the number of Jews murdered far exceeded six million. Murray saw firsthand that many Jews were not even registered when they arrived at Auschwitz. They were rushed to the gas chambers to make room for the next batch of arrivals. Unfortunately, there are no records or memories of these nameless victims.

Murray loved America. He always wore an American flag pin on his shirt collar and proudly displayed an American flag in his home. He was proud to be an American, for it was the Americans who saved him.

In 1991, I took my then 10-year-old son, Roy, to visit Uncle Murray and Aunt Rose, and I will never forget one incident. We were walking on the boardwalk in Santa Monica, California, as a soldier dressed in a U.S. military uniform approached us. Once we were within arm's length of him, my uncle bent down, kissed the soldier's shoes, reached in his pocket, and gave the soldier a hundred-dollar bill.

Astonished, probably thinking my uncle was crazy, the soldier asked, "Why are you giving me this money?"

My uncle replied, "The Americans saved my life. That is something one doesn't forget. G-d bless you, and G-d bless America."

My son, the soldier, and I were speechless. My uncle displayed an unmasked, profound hatred for the Nazis while at the same time showing an everlasting love for Americans.

Aunt Rose and Uncle Murray enjoyed their daily walks and activities. Uncle Murray learned to play chess and enjoyed playing with other European survivors. They socialized with their friends frequently and enjoyed dining out and going to the movies.

They lived happily until Aunt Rose's passing in 1992.

Uncle Murray lived another four years after Aunt Rose's death. He was a heartbroken but courageous and inspiring Holocaust survivor who felt strongly that the story of more than six million murdered Jews must live on.

He always told us, "Knowledge is strength."

Murray was peacefully laid to rest in the sprawling hills of Los Angeles, California, in 1996—far away from the burning chimneys. With him was buried the number 31321—along with the hardships, pain, and suffering no human being should ever experience.

Murray Scheinberg as a soldier in the Polish army.

UNITED STATES HOLOCAUST MEMORIAL MUSEUM

Holocaust Survivors and Victims Database

Displaying 1 of 1

Morris Scheinberg

Sex: Male

Date of Birth: 11 Jul 1911

Place of Birth: Warsaw (Poland), Russia / Soviet Russia

Religion:

- orthodox Judaism (Prewar) [Jew]
- Judaism (Wartime) [Jew]

Persecution Category: Jew

Camp:

- Dachau (Germany : Concentration Camp)
- Auschwitz II-Birkenau (Poland : Death Camp)
- Sachsenhausen (Germany : Concentration Camp)
- Auschwitz (Poland : Concentration Camp)(generic)
- Oranienburg-Heinkelwerke (Germany : Concentration Camp)

Place Hidden: Dachau (Germany)

Type of Place Hidden: buildings

Place of Liberation: Dachau (Germany)

Liberated By: armed forces / United States

Worksheet: Jewish Survivor

Notes:

- Went into Hiding

Murray's hometown of Warsaw, Poland, almost completely destroyed by the Germans. *(Warsaw Uprising Museum, Warsaw, Poland, 2013.)*

The last remaining building from the former ghetto in Warsaw, Poland. The posters on the building depict victims of the Holocaust. The building was scheduled to be demolished in 2016 to make room for condominiums.

Marilyn Shimon, author, at the main entrance to Auschwitz. Notice the inverted letter "B" on the word ARBEIT. A Jewish blacksmith deliberately inverted it as a sign of resistance. It went undetected by the Nazis.

Block 11—Solitary confinement cell in Auschwitz.

Entrance to Birkenau, 2013.

Remains of a crematorium at Auschwitz. The Germans attempted to destroy the evidence as the Allies approached in 1945.

Top (left to right): Uncle Murray, Aunt Rose, Sheldon Hirsch (author's brother), and Lisa Zolle (author's cousin) in Los Angeles, 1980. **Bottom** (left to right): Aunt Rose, Uncle Murray, and Aunt Judy in Los Angeles, 1980.

Roy Shimon (author's son), Aunt Rose and Uncle Murray, 1989.

Historical Information

During the years 1939–1945, my uncle was imprisoned at Pawiak prison, Tarnow prison, Auschwitz–Birkenau, Sachsenhausen and Dachau. A brief description is provided below about these facilities.

PAWIAK PRISON

The Pawiak prison was built in 1835 in Warsaw, Poland. It was originally used as a transfer camp for Polish inmates sentenced to be deported to Siberia. During World War II, it became part of the Nazi concentration camp apparatus.

Approximately 100,000 men and 200,000 women passed through the prison gates. Over 37,000 were executed and 60,000 were sent to concentration or death camps.

On August 21, 1945, the remaining prisoners were shot and the buildings were demolished by the Nazis.

It was not rebuilt after the war. The only remaining structure is a detention cell, which is currently used as a museum.

TARNOW

Tarnow is a Polish city located approximately 70 miles east of Krakow. The prison was situated in the center of town. Prior to World War II, 25,000 Jews lived there. Their presence went back to the 15th century. Jews were mainly employed in the garment industry. Germans occupied Tarnow in September 1939 and implemented the horrendous harassment of the Jews.

On June 14, 1940, German authorities organized the first mass transport of inmates, consisting of 728 Polish prisoners, from Tarnow prison to Auschwitz concentration camp.

The Nazis confiscated Jewish property, torched the synagogues, and required Jews to wear the Jewish Star of David patch on their clothes. A *Judenrat* [Jewish council] enforced special taxes on the Jews and provided the Germans with workers for forced labor. A ghetto was established in March 1941 and remained open for three months. On June 9, 1942, the Jews were ordered to appear at Targowica square to register for deportation. On June 11, Jews were dragged to a forest and shot. Others were shot in front of the fence at the Jewish cemetery. Additionally, Jews were deported to Belzec death camp and sent to the gas chambers.

In 1943, Jews were led from the center of town to the railroad station and transported to Auschwitz. Subsequently, Tarnow was declared *Judenrein* [free of Jews].

The Nazi occupation of Tarnow ended on January 18, 1945, when the Soviet Army entered the town.

In 1975, a monument was erected in front of the former public bathhouse, commemorating the departure of the first transport to Auschwitz.

AUSCHWITZ–BIRKENAU

The Auschwitz concentration camp complex was the largest of the camps established by the Nazi regime. It was located 37 miles west of Krakow, Poland, in the city of Oswiecim, surrounded by beautiful countryside, flowers, and flourishing trees, well hidden from the public. More than 8,000 of Oswiecim's 12,000 residents were Jewish in 1939. By 1945, there were no Jews left in the town.

Initially, Auschwitz was thought to be a model German town. Germans thought they would be returning to their homeland. Much historical evidence shows that Auschwitz actually was a German city during the Middle Ages. Auschwitz was said to be founded by Germany in 1270. When Germany incorporated Oswiecim into the Third Reich, they changed the name to Auschwitz.

In 1940, Auschwitz was chosen to be a protective-custody camp for Polish political prisoners. It was situated in a convenient location, easily accessible, had a labor exchange, and was a viable Polish military site.

As history unfolded, the camp expanded, and Auschwitz II–Birkenau was built as a death camp. Auschwitz III–Buna (Monowitz) was added as an industrial conglomeration with the German chemical company IG Farben. Over the years, the Nazis deported people from all over Europe to Auschwitz. It evolved into a complex network of camps where Jews, and anyone perceived as enemies of the Reich, were exterminated.

Mass killings of the Jews continued at the complex until its liberation in 1945.

Despite the heinous acts that occurred at Auschwitz II–Birkenau, many Jews did rebel. In fact, 144 Jews escaped during the five years of operation. The notorious inscription above the main entrance to Auschwitz, *"ARBEIT MACHT FREI,"* is one example of how Jews defied the Nazis. The Nazis had ordered several Jewish blacksmith prisoners to make the sign. In doing so, they deliberately turned the *B* in the word *ARBEIT* upside down, as an indication of resistance and defiance. The inverted *B* was to become a message to always remember the tragedies that took place on the other side of the sign. In January of 1945, the Germans realized that Soviet forces were approaching the camp complex and ordered the camp to be abandoned. The SS immediately began evacuating over 60,000 prisoners by forcing them to march 30 kilometers west to Gliwice. These marches became known as the *death marches*. SS guards shot anyone who could not keep up the pace. Prisoners were cold, barely able to walk, and suffered from malnutrition. Many died during the marches.

The Nazis blew up buildings and destroyed records in an attempt to rid themselves of the evidence of their heinous crimes.

In January of 1945, the Soviet Army entered the camps and liberated 7,600 nonhuman-looking prisoners. They found piles of corpses, thousands of articles of clothing, shoes, eyeglasses, and seven tons of human hair, among other articles that the Germans didn't have time to dispose of.

Officially, the records state that 1.1 million people were murdered at Auschwitz, but there were more deaths of unregistered Jews. 85 percent of those murdered there were Jewish.

Auschwitz was the center of the mass murder of the Jews and has become a symbol of evil that generates from racism and national chauvinism.

SACHSENHAUSEN

Sachsenhausen, located north of Berlin, was built in 1936 by prisoners from Emsland concentration camp, specifically for incarcerating political prisoners. It was expected to be an ideal camp and an important component of the concentration system. SS officers were sent to the camp for training purposes.

More than 200,000 people were incarcerated at Sachsenhausen between 1936 and 1945: Jews, Sinti, Roma, and homosexuals.

Several tens of thousands of people were murdered at the camp. They died of hunger, exhaustion, illnesses, and public executions. Medical experiments were conducted at the camp, including castrations and sterilizations. Deportations to Dachau were frequent.

In 1942, more than 12,000 Soviet prisoners of war and Jews were killed during a test of gassing vehicles and an installation for shooting prisoners in the back of their necks.

By 1945, 80,000 men, women, and children were held prisoner in the camp. On February 1, 1945, as the Red Army approached, the commandant gave orders to evacuate the camp. Those not fit to march were murdered. By February 13, 1945, 16,000 prisoners reached the Belowerwald (currently used as a museum). On April 1, 1945, 30,000 prisoners were divided into groups of 500 and marched northwest.

Prisoners arrived at Schwerin, where they encountered the Red Army and were liberated.

On April 22, 1945, Soviet Union troops liberated the camp. They found 3,000 ill prisoners remaining. These were the ones who were too weak to participate in the death marches.

The camp was disbanded on April 29, 1945. A memorial stands at its site.

DACHAU

The first of the Nazi concentration camps opened in the town of Dachau, 10 miles northwest of Munich, in 1933. It was built on the grounds of an abandoned munitions factory. It was intended as a facility for forced labor. It became the prototype for future concentration camps. Theodor Eicke, the commandant of the camp in 1933, demanded complete obedience from the officers and guards. The camp layout and routine were copied at the other camps. In fact, SS guards were trained at Dachau. Throughout the years, it grew to include 100 sub camps—mostly *Arbeitskommandos* [work camps]. Many prisoners were assigned tasks such as building roads, working in gravel pits, and draining the marshes. The camp administrator was located at the gatehouse at the main entrance. An electrified barbed-wire fence and seven watchtowers surrounded the camp. Prisoners lived in constant fear of brutal treatment, detention in standing cells, flogging, or pole hanging. The camp was divided into two sections: the camp grounds and the crematoria area. There were specific barracks for clergy as well as for the medical experiments conducted on the premises. German physicians conducted experiments on the prisoners, including high altitude tests and malaria and hypothermia experiments.

As Allied forces advanced towards Germany, Nazis at Dachau began moving the prisoners out of the camp in an attempt to prevent their liberation. They traveled for days without food or water. Approximately 7,000 Jews were ordered to go on a death march to the town of Tegernsee.

Nearly 188,000 people were incarcerated at Dachau from 1933 to 1945. On April 26, 1945, there were 67,665 registered prisoners—including 22,100 Jews. There were 32,000 documented deaths at the camp.

Dachau was liberated on Sunday, April 29, 1945, one week before the end of World War II, by the US Seventh Army, the 42nd Rainbow Division, and the 45th Thunderbird Division, with the added support of the 290th Armored Division.

The Germans surrendered near the gate next to the prison enclosure. SS soldiers came forth holding a white flag. The Americans found an abandoned train outside the camp with over 2,301 dead bodies in it.

After the war, the Dachau facility was used to detain SS soldiers awaiting trial. From 1948 until its closure in 1960, the United States used Dachau as a military base.

Although the gates of the camps have been closed for years, many Nazis continue to proclaim they were *just following orders.*

Sources

Dlugoborski, Waclaw. *Auschwitz 1940–1945*. Oswiecim: Auschwitz-Birkenau State Museum, 2000.

Friedrich, Otto. *The Kingdom of Auschwitz*. New York: Harper Perennial, 1982.

Hirshaut, Julien. *Jewish Martyrs of Pawiak*. New York: Holocaust Publications, 1982.

Holocaust Memorial Day Trust, *22/04/1945: Liberation of Sachsenhausen Concentration Camp*. hnd.org.uk/content/2204145-liberation-sachsenhausen-concentration-camp.

United States Holocaust Memorial Museum, *Tarnow*, accessed January 29, 2016. http://www.ushmm.org/wlc/mobile/en/article/Tarnow.

United States Holocaust Memorial Museum, *Establishment of the Dachau Camp*, accessed January 29, 2016. http://www.ushmn.org/wlc/mobile/en/article.php?Moduleld=1005214.

Chronology

January 30, 1933

Hitler is appointed chancellor of Germany.

March 33, 1933

First concentration camp, Dachau, opens near Munich, Germany.

April 1, 1933

Boycott of Jewish-owned stores and businesses in Germany.

August 2, 1934

President of Germany, Paul von Hindenburg, dies. Hitler becomes president and commander-in-chief of the armed forces.

March 17, 1935

German Army enters Rhineland.

September 15, 1935

Nuremberg Laws are passed, denying Jews citizenship in Germany.

March 13, 1938

Germany invades Austria.

August 17, 1938

German Jewish women must add "Sara" to their
name and men must add "Israel."

November 7, 1938

Herschel Grynszpan, a Jew, kills a German diplomat
in Paris.

November 9, 1938

Kristallnacht [The Night of Broken Glass]—267
synagogues are burned, 7,500 Jewish businesses are
vandalized, 91 Jews are murdered, and 30,000 Jews
are sent to concentration camps.

March 15, 1939

Germany occupies Czechoslovakia.

August 23, 1939

Nazi–Soviet pact is signed, agreeing not to attack each
other.

September 1, 1939

Germany invades Poland. World War II begins.

September 3, 1939

England and France declare war on Germany.

September 21, 1939

Ghettos are established in Poland.

April 9, 1940

Germany invades Denmark and Norway.

May 10, 1940

Germany invades Holland, Belgium, and France.

April 27, 1940

Auschwitz concentration camp is established.

April 6, 1941

Germany invades Yugoslavia and Greece.

October 8, 1941

Construction of Auschwitz II–Birkenau death camp begins.

November, 1940

Warsaw ghetto is established.

June 22, 1941

Germany attacks the Soviet Union. *Einsatzgruppen* [firing squads] begin mass killings of Soviet Jews.

September 28, 1941

More than 30,000 Jews at Babi Yar, Ukraine, are murdered by shootings.

December 7, 1941

Japan attacks Pearl Harbor.

December 8, 1941

United States declares war on Germany.

December 11, 1941

Germany and Italy declare war on the United States.

January 20, 1942

Wannsee Conference takes place, and plans for the Final Solution and total destruction of the Jews are outlined.

June 1, 1942

Treblinka death camp opens.

April 19, 1943

Warsaw ghetto revolt begins.

May, 1944

Over 400,000 Hungarian Jews are murdered at Auschwitz.

June 6, 1944

Allies land at Normandy, France—D-Day.

July 24, 1944

Soviet forces discover Majdanek death camp.

October 4, 1944

Revolt in Auschwitz takes place.

April 15, 1945

Britain liberates Bergen-Belsen. Anne Frank died there several weeks before liberation.

April 29, 1945

American troops liberate Dachau concentration camp.

April 30, 1945

Adolf Hitler commits suicide.

May 8, 1945

Germany surrenders.

November 22, 1945

International military war-crimes trials begin (Nuremberg Trials).

Uncle Murray's Chronology

July 11, 1911

Born in Warsaw as Moishe.

December 3, 1939

Arrested and imprisoned for interrogation in Pawiak prison in Warsaw.

December 11, 1939

Transferred to the regular prison in Tarnow, Poland, and incarcerated as an opponent of occupied Nazi regime.

June 14, 1940

Transferred to KL Auschwitz concentration camp as a political prisoner.

November 29, 1943

Transferred to Auschwitz II–Birkenau and registered as number 31321.

November 2, 1944

Transferred to Sachsenhausen concentration camp with a brief stopover in Oranienburg.

November 17, 1944

Transferred to Dachau concentration camp.

April 17, 1945

Escapes Dachau.

April 29, 1945

Liberated by the US Seventh Army's 45th Infantry.

May 8, 1946

Marries Sonya Beder at the Displaced Persons camp.

February 27, 1947

Sonya and Mondig immigrate to the United States and have one son.

1960

Murray and Sonya divorce.

1963

Murray meets Rose Kodimer.

1996

Murray Scheinberg is laid to rest in Los Angeles, California.

About the Author

Marilyn Shimon is a Holocaust educator and volunteer Gallery Educator at the Museum of Jewish Heritage—A Living Memorial to the Holocaust, in New York.

A retired New York City schoolteacher, Shimon has a certificate in Holocaust and Genocide Studies from the Jan Karski Institute for Holocaust Education at Georgetown University and holds degrees from NYU and Hofstra University. She earned a 2016 scholarship from the Center for Judaic, Holocaust and Peace Studies at Appalachian State University. Shimon is an alumna of the Holocaust &

Jewish Resistance Teachers' program and participated in the ninth annual Charlotte and Jacques Wolf Educators' Conference with the Anti-Defamation League.

The mayor of Jerusalem recognized Shimon for her work as a volunteer soldier in the Yom Kippur War. She taught English and music in Israel. Serving as a translator for the Israel Ministry of Defense in New York, she was involved in meetings leading up to the Camp David Accords.

Shimon lives in New York, where her son, Roy, is an attorney.